LIVING OUT MY SECOND CHANCE

Triumphing Over Cancer Day by Day

By

Dan A. Colachicco

Dan Colachicco
P.O. Box 951764
Lake Mary, Florida 32795
Email: *DColachicco@CommercialEdge.com*

ISBN: 978-0-692-03391-3

Dedication

To Nancy. There would be no life for me without you. You are the source of all things good in my life and the reason I want to live. Through this, you were the foundation that kept me strong, the energy that made me fight, the laughter that gave me joy and the arms that held me up. You are my personal survival kit. To say "I love you" is not enough. You are my life, my hope, my joy, my heart, my soul and my entire world.

Diagnosis

Introduction

Today is Columbus Day; a holiday for government workers, postal delivery folks and school children among others. For those who aren't required to be at work or school, they are enjoying a carefree extended weekend day. I wasn't able to do that today.

You see, last Thursday, October the 4th at approximately 10:00 a.m., I found out that I have colon cancer. In the 5 to 10 minutes leading up to that discovery, I had just undergone a colonoscopy, and was telling my beautiful wife, Nancy, of 31 years that nurses want you to fart after having a colonoscopy, and by the way, where was she going to take me to breakfast?

Our mood became dramatically more somber after my physician, Dr. Weinstein, unceremoniously plopped a series of ugly photos on my lap, simultaneously explaining that I indeed had a cancerous tumor inside of me. The doctor also expressed concerns about more than a dozen other polyps that were malignant. Most of that conversation is still a blur. I heard his words, but it was hard to put them together in a way that made sense.

Dr. Weinstein sprung into action and sent me to our local diagnostic imaging center for an outpatient "stat" CT Scan. (I don't like that word "stat." I didn't like the word before I got cancer.) The Doctor wastes no time in scheduling an appointment first thing the next morning at the "Florida Hospital Cancer Center in Orlando" to undergo genetic testing. So much for breakfast.

While sitting next to my wife in the car, I began trying to process the information I had been given, what it meant, and it's consequences. I was trying to get my head, heart and emotions to make sense so that I could figure out what was happening to me. I simply could not escape the movies that were playing inside of my head. The movies were the story of my life, and they all were ending tragically. I wanted to stay positive, and for short periods of time, I could stay composed. But the anxiety, fear, and dread would again start knocking on my mind's door, and I would feel my world spin out of control. I wanted to feel normal again.

I was told that my doctor would have the results of the CT Scan by late Friday afternoon. I waited for that information, knowing that it would give me the answer as to whether cancer had spread from the tumor to other part parts of my body. That phone call was essential to my very existence. Friday went by, and the phone call never came.

In fact, the whole weekend goes by without me knowing if the tumor permeated other parts of my body. What if the tumor had already spread? What will they do then? What about my life? What is my fate?

My doctor gave me medication to take for anxiety during this time, and it did help a little. What helped me the most was holding tightly to the people and the things that projected positive energy for me to absorb. I received that energy from my wife.

My wife Nancy is the best. There is simply no one I have ever known who is capable of such love and support. Throughout that weekend, we talked. We spoke in the way two people talk when they know and love each other. I bore my rawest emotions, and my wife held me up. Nancy was there for me.

Connecting with my wife also made me feel the need to reconnect with God. I have had an on again/off again relationship with Catholicism. I grew up in a Catholic family, so it makes sense that I feel the need to re-engage with that faith.

I have a rosary that I got at the 1964 World's Fair in New York. It had supposedly been blessed by a Bishop or a Cardinal, or some other high-ranking holy guy representing God. But the truth is, I actually had to go online and look up how to say a rosary. I did the best I could and spoke to Him from the heart. With that rosary in my hand, I prayed with all my might. I asked

God for a positive outcome from the tests, for strength, and for the healing that would allow me more time on this earth. I promised God that if He answered my prayers, I would vow to be a better person, strive to improve myself, and would live a more fulfilling life. I would live a life that would be of benefit to my loved ones. I didn't know what life changes all of these promises would entail but I knew that if He could just give me a second chance, I would figure it out. I would not let Him down. That's all I want, a second chance.

Now, on this beautiful Columbus Day, I am trying to stay focused on positive things and live out this day as normally as possible. I am determined not to let my anxiety overwhelm me. I hit the gym at 7:00 a.m. I notice that I'm not putting the time constraints on myself that I usually do when I am at the gym. As ridiculous as it is, I am a clock-watcher when I work out. I always feel that time is taking me away from something else I *should* be doing. Today, I'm just going to enjoy my workout, and I'm going to stay as long as I feel like it. Is this step one of the new me? I don't know, but I like it.

I've always heard about how news like "you have cancer" changes the way you see things in life, but right now I'm really starting to see what that means. A list of the important things in my life is clearer than ever before. It is like there is a flashing neon sign in my brain telling me, "Hey asshole, here's the real list:" The sign begins to flash on and off with the important things that I now know to be true. The love you share with your wife and sons. The beauty of your home. Your good health that allows you to enjoy your friends who care about you. The precious gift of time. That list is still growing.

As I sit with my wife enjoying coffee talk and anticipating "the call," she gasps and looks out our back window. "*Look at that beautiful red cardinal that just landed on the pool screen,*" she exclaimed. I got up from my chair and looked. I have never seen a cardinal more red and beautiful than this one staring back at me through the glass door. Actually, I've never seen a cardinal around our house that I can remember. The reason this moment between me and the beautiful red cardinal is important is that my mother absolutely loved cardinals, and she had pictures and ceramics of them all over her house. Immediately upon seeing this little fella, a vision of my mom popped into my head, and I think I smiled. Trying to keep the positive emotions percolating in my head, I told myself that maybe, just perhaps, mom was stopping by to say that everything was going to be okay.

The rest of the morning lumbered along, and I began to wonder if the Doctor's offices were closed for the holiday. I had no plans to call them. Then Nancy came home from the grocery store with determination in her eyes that I haven't seen too many times before. She called the doctor, and within a few minutes, I had the results I had been waiting for. "*There is nothing in the report that indicates that the cancer has spread." The Dr. will call you later to discuss it with you".* I don't think I will ever forget those words. No matter how much you think you know yourself, the emotions you hold deep within you have a life of their own. If the news had been bad, I would have fully expected to experience a complete meltdown. I had anticipated that if the news were good, I'd be doing fist pumps, somersaults, rebel yells and the like, all with a big grin on my face. But, that is not what happened.

I wept. I wept uncontrollably. I wept in my wife's arms. I wept into my clammy hands. I wept into my lap. I wept on my clothes, napkins, furniture, you name it. It was "Weepapalooza." I really didn't realize the depth of emotions that had pent up inside of me. We passed the news along to friends and family. And that was nice.

I even told Nancy about Cardinal mom. Things settled down, and Nancy left for her appointments and her daily visit with her mother. I walked out into the backyard and looked for that cardinal. He (or she) wasn't around, but I realized that my prayers had been heard and answered. There will be more prayers to come as I face the surgery and treatment which, as of this writing is still unknown to me, but it doesn't look like the movie is going to have the tragic end I feared. So it's time to remember the things I said in my prayers.

Jimmy Buffett tells the story of how he almost died when his seaplane flipped over on take-off. From that experience, he penned a line in the song Far Side of the World that says ***"Time to Sing, Time to Dance, Living Out My Second Chance."*** In the past 48 hours or so, I asked God to please just give me a second chance. It looks like he is going to come through for me, and I am very grateful. I don't sing or dance very well, and the only time I actually do those things is when I'm *at* a Jimmy Buffett concert, but it's time to start living out *my* second chance.

In these pages, I'll keep you up to date on my progress, day by day. I've started to write out a life plan for how I intend to keep my promise to God. I wasn't sure what the list would look like when I prayed for my second chance, but if my prayers were answered, I'd come up with some doozies. So these aren't in any particular order. I'm just writing as they come into my head and my heart.

- I will cherish the moments I share with family and friends in the effort to preserve them as memories. This will be the most important focus of my life.
- I will take responsibility for my good health every day.
- I will live more simply and focus on decreasing clutter in my life. I will learn to optimize my time.

- I will make Nancy aware of all of our personal responsibilities so that we are ready for anything.
- I will assemble an action plan and a team of people I trust to support Nancy if I am suddenly incapacitated or out of the picture.
- I will not be afraid.
- I will make good memories for Nancy and my loved ones.
- I will not yell. I'm an Italian, so I may make wild hand gestures, but I will not yell.
- I will not lose my temper. My kids will love this one.
- I will always show appreciation to those who help me.
- I will not be judgmental.
- I will be more focused on how precious every minute is.
- I will balance work, home, family, and friends. When I am not working, I will be fully present with the people I love and attend to the friendships I value.
- I will ignore the truly unimportant and meaningless things that used to cause me stress. There are so many of these.
- I will create the permanent financial stability that will survive me.
- I will enjoy time and activities with my precious sons.

- I will be more tolerant, less critical, and learn to take criticism well.
- I will not be a slave to time. Working out at the gym, enjoying our home, relaxing when I eat…
- I will pray regularly and be grateful for my health and my blessings.
- I will have a positive impact on peoples' lives and expect nothing in return. Karma man.
- I will take every opportunity to engage in random acts of kindness.
- I will smile in the mirror first thing in the morning. This might sound goofy as hell, but I have learned that you cannot feel down or negative when you have a big silly smile on your face.
- I will fill my brain with positive images.
- I will define success beyond the scope of money.
- I will make people laugh. Hopefully, this will include me.
- I will reach out to people whom I can help.
- I will monitor my happiness and decide to be happy in every moment. The thought of happiness as a decision is kind of cool.
- I will think bigger picture.
- I will take nothing for granted.
- I will set life goals and achieve them
- I will appreciate the people who care about me and let them know it.
- I will never refuse to contribute to a kid's request for a donation or sale.

- I will face the truth without fear.
- I will pay sincere compliments at every opportunity.
- I will make sure Nancy and the kids know I love them every single day.
- I will not rush. Nancy is never going to believe this one.
- I will not assume anything.
- I will not hold grudges. This will come from the Irish part of my heritage.
- I will pause for sunrises and reflect on each sunset
- I will not procrastinate.
- I will learn to speak Italian fluently. This means knowing more than the menu at my favorite restaurant or just the curse words.
- I will surround myself with positive people and positive ideals.
- I will read uplifting books.

I've found the reactions from people I've told about my cancer to be very sobering. It must just be that "C" word. If you tell someone "I have the flu," they seldom say "you'll be in our thoughts and prayers." Don't get me wrong, I appreciate being in anyone's thoughts and prayers. I'll take all the positive energy I can muster from every source. I think the statement reflects everyone's perception of how frightening the diagnosis is to most people. And I get it. Hear the "C" word, and everyone automatically assumes the worst. I wish it weren't so grave. I've had a few people say to me, “I’m not worried about you; I know you’ll beat it.” I like that. But if I could coach people who are told that their friend or a loved one has been diagnosed with cancer, I would advise them against the “thoughts and prayers” comment. It’s way overused anyway. I’d tell them to say something like “What can I do for you right now, or this week, or anytime, to help?

When said in sincerity, showing that you are there to provide support to your friend or a loved one is probably just as important as being in their thoughts and prayers. Be where their feet are… in the present. Provide support in real time. Thoughts and prayers are comforting but can seem one step removed from them.

I am scared shitless about the whole process: surgery, what they are going to find once they get in there, the accuracy of the tests, etc. It seems to be 90% of what I think about these days, and that is not pleasant. But overall, I’m starting to feel like there will indeed be a normal life to reflect on in a few weeks once this is over. That is certainly a far cry from October 4th, 2012, which was undeniably the worst day of my life. So I am truly grateful for the thoughts and prayers as I go through this. But I’d like to know that I can still have them when this is over, and I’m moving on with my life. In return, I plan to keep more people in my thoughts and prayers as well.

October 4th, 2012

Once the initial body blow started to fade, the people that I felt needed to know what was going on with me began to permeate my mind. I was utterly distraught at the idea of telling my sons, yet I did feel the need to tell someone. I'm not really sure why I felt that way. I think I wanted to hear from friends and loved ones that everything was going to be alright. But the reality of my situation was that everything was definitely not alright.

We arrived at the diagnostic imaging facility where I would be getting my "stat" CT scan to help determine if this cancer had spread. Nancy dealt with all of the annoying logistics involved with insurance and paperwork. This was a process that I would be repeating innumerable times over the next several months. While she was navigating the paperwork maze, I decided to call my closest friend in the world, Russ.

Calling Russ a friend is an understatement. I don't know what it's like to have a brother, but sharing some DNA cannot make two men closer than Russ and I. We have been friends for more than 30 years, and I don't think we have ever had a cross word between us. On this particular day, Russ answered the phone with a demented comment about all the joys of a colonoscopy procedure. I could not hold back the tears as I said, "listen to me very carefully. I'm not bullshitting you. I have colon cancer." Russ was very stoic in his response. He suggested getting a second opinion and then questioned if the diagnosis might be a mistake. Then, as I should have expected, he said "I'm leaving now. I'll be there in 3 hours." I convinced Russ that he didn't need to come right now and that Nancy and I needed some time to process exactly what colon cancer is, and how it was going to affect our lives. Russ answered simply and with sincerity, "We will get through this together." And just like a brother, he repeatedly made good on that promise over the next few months.

This incredible friend of mine runs a successful business and doesn't have a lot of extra time to spare. Yet, he made a split-second decision that nothing was more important than being by my side. The decision a brother would make. He lives 200 miles away from me yet would come to visit me whenever I was in the hospital as if it was just around the corner from where he lived.

As the time passed and I reflected on the important people in my life, I came to realize that Russ is the definition of a true friend. As it relates to my situation, a true friend is someone who loves you to the point that, if given the opportunity, they would trade places with you. I know that Russ is that strong of a friend. He tirelessly researched cures, alternative treatments, and holistic remedies. He accompanied me on my first appointment with the surgeon and offered to go with me on every other appointment I had. He made me laugh when I felt like crying, and he helped me see a future that was hard for me to see under the circumstances. He encouraged me, he stayed involved, and his compassion was limitless. This friendship of a lifetime is one of the most valuable experiences I have known. Yes, Russ is my brother.

Next, it was time to tell my sons. How do you tell your kids that they very likely may be losing their father? YOU DON'T. I must be confident and give them hope. I want to be the one to tell them, myself, in my words. Can I do this without having another meltdown? I have to. An emotional collapse would send the opposite of the message that I want to send. I need to conjure up all of my emotional strength to make these calls and deliver the news in such a way that my precious sons will not experience the fear that I am feeling. I am sure they will have their private conversations with each other and with their mother, but it was time to call both of them and let them know what was going on.

My boys are both extraordinary but very different. I would call Billy first. He is very spiritual and is able to think in abstract concepts. That is probably a good thing since he is getting ready to be hit with some bad news that will have no resolution in the months to come. He doesn't answer.

I leave him a message with some sense of urgency and send him a text. He calls back in 2 minutes. Somehow, God gave me the strength and peace of mind I needed to remain calm. It was much easier for me to break the news to him than I anticipated.

"We got some bad news today pal," I said calmly without becoming over-emotional. "They found a tumor in my colon, and it is cancerous. I am going to have to go through some stuff here to get better." That's pretty abstract, right? Billy became a little pensive but basically just acknowledged everything I said without asking any questions. That is his style. I knew he was going to process all of this and then come up with his own list of questions and conclusions. Billy said I shouldn't worry, and reassured me in a confident and sincere voice that he felt sure everything was going to be fine. The entire call probably lasted less than 2 minutes. Billy is a man of few words.

After calling Billy, I realized that I could garner some control over my emotions. Now it was time to call Anthony who is far more animated, inquisitive, and tends to say whatever pops into his head.

I need to be ready to think on my feet before I call him. He will probably ask more questions and want to get answers on the spot. Anthony inherited my lack of patience. I call, and he picks up after the first ring with a hearty "Hey what's up?" My delivery is pretty much the same as when I told Billy. "The colonoscopy didn't go too well, pal. They found a cancerous tumor, and I'll have to have surgery to get rid of it. They scheduled a bunch of tests to see how bad it is so I really don't know at this point." I figured I'd try to answer a lot of the questions I knew he wanted to ask before he had the chance to ask them.

"Really," he said with emphasis. "I'm not worried about you. You'll be fine."

Despite the positive words, I could hear the concern in his voice, and I knew he was just trying to make me feel better. After we had hung up, it would not have surprised me if he had immediately called Nan to talk to her about it further. He didn't, but I know that call was not going to be long in coming.

After finishing the painful chore of telling my sons that I had cancer, I turned my thoughts to how great it would be to tell them that I was cured. I could feel a glimmer of hope even though I had nothing tangible to base it on. I want that. I want to have the joy of telling people that I am ok. That I am going to live. I want it. I want it very badly, and I am going to fight to get to that day.

October 10, 2012

I've had several people tell me that there is a surgeon in town who is one of the best in the world for colon cancer. Hs name is Dr. Matthews. Ironically, my friend Sheila recommended him quite strongly because he was the surgeon who treated her husband and my friend Jay for liver cancer. I have been thinking about Jay a lot since this all happened. Jay died from liver cancer six months ago. I remember how shocked I was to read a Facebook post from Sheila announcing the news and making a plea to everyone and anyone for advice or alternative treatment options. When Jay died, I was so sad. It seemed to happen quickly, and I just thought that somehow he would recover from it. It didn't seem fair. Jay had a beautiful wife, an adorable little 2-year-old daughter and a successful business. He was full of life. The news of his death made me regret that I didn't go and see him earlier. I thought about Sheila and her little girl. All of it was so sad and last Thursday when I got the news I thought about Jay almost immediately. I just got the same news Jay got. Jay died a few months after getting the news.

What is going to happen to me? Do I only have a few months like Jay did? Now his widow was trying to help me by recommending a surgeon. She texted him and got me an appointment to see him immediately. I had another name to drop which was a friend of ours who works for Florida Hospital and plays golf with Dr. Matthews. I never thought I would need a cancer surgeon. Suddenly, all of these people in my life know this guy who is supposed to be one of the best for exactly the kind of cancer I have. Interesting. Maybe this is good karma or fate or something. We'll see. I am definitely going to get another opinion, probably more than one.

My appointment to see Dr. Matthews is at 5:00 p.m. He wants me to bring the CD of the scan I had done which I picked up this morning. Russ drove up, and he is going to the appointment with me. Nancy is in New York with her best friend seeing Barbra Streisand in Brooklyn. There was no way I was going to let her miss that. I'll have to make a call to her after my appointment and let her know what the doctor said. I hope it isn't bad news. If it is, it will ruin her trip. Then again if the news is good, she will have some peace of mind and be able to enjoy herself. I am thinking positive, but I am nervous as hell. Russ is with me trying to make me laugh and telling me that everything is going to work out fine. I appreciate him so much, and I know his heart is in the right place, but if the news is bad I want to be alone. I don't want to burden other people I care about with sadness and worrying. I want to take that on myself. In my own way and without any fanfare. Sometimes the best support you can get is being left alone and thinking things through without outside influences. This feels like one of those times.

I fill out all of the paperwork at Dr. Matthews's very modest office. It feels like I have filled out a zillion of these forms lately. They are all starting to look the same. The nurse calls my name and asks Russ if he wants to come back with me to see the doctor. He answers "of course." I am glad to have his support, but I want to be able to focus on what the doctor is saying. I have a lot of questions but am scared to hear the answers. I don't want Russ to share the brunt of bad news, and I sure don't want him to see me break down which has happened a few times in the past week. It doesn't matter though because the two of us are now marching back to Dr. Matthews's office.

Dr. Matthews is a very busy man. He is multi-tasking even as he starts talking to us, with the nurse giving him papers to sign and his wife texting him to not be late for their son's soccer game. At the same time, he is talking to me. We very briefly mention Jay and Sheila, a subject that seems to be required to discuss since Sheila got me the appointment, but neither of us really wants to have a conversation about it.

I drop the name of our friend from Florida Hospital, and he smiles. Then it is right down to business. He is looking at the scan and talking to himself. I have no idea what he is talking about. He is saying something about centimeters and it being higher or lower but nothing that indicates if anything he is looking at is good or bad. He abruptly stops and says “Ok let’s go have a look at this thing.” He gets up out of his chair and heads for the door and gives me a “what are you waiting for” kind of look. We go to an exam room, and he proceeds to conduct what I can only describe as an incredibly invasive examination.

We went back to his office where Russ was sitting in the same relaxed position he was in when I walked out. I glanced at him, and he looked back with a nervous inquisitive look. His eyes darted between Dr.Matthews and me. I could tell Russ was waiting for some sort of definitive diagnosis from the exam that just took place.

Dr. Matthews barely sat down in his chair before he grabbed a blank piece of paper and darted over to our side of the desk. He sat between Russ and me, and he was talking a mile a minute. I was struggling to keep up. I wanted to hear and understand every word that came out of this mouth. He was using medical terms that I didn’t understand, and he was using them very matter of factly as though everyone should know what those words meant. He put the blank sheet of white paper on top of his writing pad and began to draw.

"We use a less invasive robotic system that cuts way down on your recovery time. There will be five small incisions; here, here, here, here and one in your belly button. Each incision is about one and a half centimeters wide." I'm thinking, *well how long is a centimeter doc*? This is America, say it in feet and inches. Are those half-assed lines you just scribbled on the paper the actual size of the incision? Did you measure how many freaking centimeters wide they are? He's still talking at warp speed, so I decide I will look up how long a centimeter is after I leave. For now, I will settle for the big picture and listen to the story. I need to hear the story of how this man plans on saving my life.

"There will be an incision just above your pubic line about 3 inches wide" he says. Great. Now we're back to inches. This I can visualize.

"We should be able to get good enough margin and hope for the best." I don't know if that is good or bad. "Hope for the best" doesn't sound promising. I am about to ask him what the hell that means, but he is not coming up for air. This is either just his nature or he is really anxious to get to his kid's soccer game. I want to tell him, "This is my life! Fuck the game! Slow down so I can understand what you are saying. I have questions, damn it!"

"We have three goals," the doctor says as he continues to write in a terrible cursive that I can't read. We will remove the tumor and surrounding lymph nodes leaving a large margin to be sure we got it all. Next, we hope to regain enough function with the connection of the colon to the anus to avoid a colostomy bag. Even if you need one for a while, we can probably get everything functioning to the point where it will only be temporary. The ultimate goal is that we want you to have a complete recovery, allowing you to live a normal life."

The surgeon adds, "This is assuming that when we take you to surgery, the tumor is the same as it appears now. I want you to have an MRI so that I can pinpoint exactly where this thing is. We'll set it up, okay?" And with that, the doctor begins to prepare to leave.

I came in here expecting to ask zillion questions and now is my chance. But I can't think of even one. His words come out of his mouth, and I hear them, but I can't seem to process the information I am getting. I hear, "colostomy bag…connect the colon and the anus…quick recovery…hope for the best."

Wait, what was that last thing? Did he just say "hope for the best?" That was a little weird. Well, he seems confident, and I like the short recovery idea. I also like the "live a normal life" comment. That sounds encouraging.

He didn't say I was going to die. In fact, he didn't seem to even consider it. But if he did think that dying was a possibility, would he tell me? If he thought my disease had a poor prognosis, would he be giving me false hope?

This guy must have to break the bad news to patients all the time. Common sense tells me that he isn't sugar coating the news to make me feel better. But what if this guy is planning on telling my friend Russ the real truth so that Russ can give me the bad news and soften the blow? I decide that this guy is probably shooting me straight. He is confident and comfortable with his plan of care for me and seems to know what he is doing. After all, this is his rodeo, and the sign on the door says "Colon and Rectal Surgeon." He is also highly recommended by people I know and trust, so why don't I just go ahead and accept what he told me? I can embrace those three goals. This surgeon and I want the same outcome; to get rid of this cancer and let me get on with my life.

I made a decision right then. I have the choice of what information to believe and not to believe, and I am going to choose to believe this man. I am going to push the skepticism away and trust that this is the guy who can cure me of cancer and save my life.

But no way am I leaving this office without asking a question, and I finally came up with one. I ask, "So if all of this goes the way you hope, what will be the after-effects? Am I going to be totally healthy again?

The surgeon replies, "Probably the biggest effect on your life is that you may need to poop 8 or 10 times a day for a while. You're going to lose most of your rectum during the surgery so the colon will have to do the work previously done by the rectum. Your body will need to adapt to expelling waste without the rectal muscle. You will adjust."

I realize then that the surgeon is talking regarding the future. Yes, this guy believes that this is treatable, and he is talking to me about life after the surgery. He believes I am going to make it.

I asked my question, and I got my answer. The surgeon is saying what I have prayed I would hear. I cannot wait to tell Nan.

For the first time since I got the CT scan results, I feel happy. My heart is swelling with relief, and I am starting to feel emotional again. This is going to be okay, and I am going to live. I don't want to cry in front of Russ. I am going to focus on what the doc is saying, and he is saying that I am ill, I am going to get well, and I am going to live.

"So let's get that MRI set up and then we will get you scheduled for surgery." And with that, he darts out of the room.

The guy is still talking, but not to me. At first, I hear him talking with the nurse in muffled voices, and then they are gone.

Russ immediately hits me on the arm and says, "There you go. I told you this was going to be fine." I usually can't stand someone telling me, "I told you so," but in this case, I can take it. Russ then starts to crack dirty jokes about the stuff in Dr. Matthews's office and asking why someone would choose a profession where they spend all day every day focused on people's assholes. Things are starting to feel like they are getting back to normal. Life goes on.

October 14th, 2012

I am making changes. They are little changes, but things that have a profound impact on my sense of well-being. Now that this is hanging over me, I feel like I am living inside my own head and there is a constant chatter going on. There are more "what if" scenarios and "why did this happen" dissertations than you can imagine. Knowing that I have cancer makes me want to change a lot of things. I wonder why? Sometimes I think that getting cancer was my own fault. Who else's fault could it be? It's because of what I ate. It's because I didn't control my stress. It's because I partied too hard. I can't go back and change those things, and I don't really know for sure if they had anything at all to do with me getting this disease.

I want to make changes going forward that might help me to live longer; changes that might help me fight this disease. So I find myself continually thinking about changes I can make in my life. Because it is a colon or rectal cancer (not really sure at this point), I have to look at diet first. Do I eat total shit? No. Well sometimes I do, but not often enough to definitively say that is the reason I acquired this cancer. I am going to get really strict with my diet.

I am scouring the internet for information about what I should be eating (and not eating) to fight cancer. As one might expect, there is an insane amount of information related to the subjects of diet and cancer, so there is going to be a lot of filtering to do. It is frustrating because there is a lot of conflicting information.

One "respected" nutritionist says organic fruits and vegetables should be the only things I should be eating. I guess that makes sense. But then I find another article that says not to eat fruit when you have cancer because it spikes blood sugar, and cancer feeds off of sugar. That makes sense too.

There are endless articles and ads about supplements to take and alternative medicine treatments. How the hell do I know what is right and what is voodoo? I tell myself to use common sense. I know that a lot of what I eat is packaged and processed and that can't be good. So there is a place to start. I'll figure out the rest as I go, but from now on I am going to try to eat real food that isn't from a package with a bunch of shit that I can't pronounce on the ingredients label.

I've been making fun of Russ for eating "liquid weeds" which is some concoction of greens, fruits and a bunch of powdered shit blended up to look like something you put on your lawn. Maybe that is what I should be eating every day. I read about this Gerson guy who supposedly figured out how to cure cancer with a liquid diet of just fruits and veggies. Sounds whacky but I am open to anything.

In addition to diet, I am trying to get my stress under control. I found a light jazz station on the radio, and that is all I listen to now. At first, it actually feels like it makes things worse because I have the urge to find a song that I can turn up to warp 10 and sing along with. But I am trying to calm things down in my head so I just let the soft music kind of wash over me. After a few minutes, it starts to feel a bit more relaxing. I didn't think it would be so much work to relax, but I am handling it. Once it kicks in it feels good.

My son the super-spiritual, metaphysically enlightened, Buddha-studying scholar recommends meditation. I look on iTunes and find these podcasts that do "guided meditation." Guided is when there is some guy or some gal telling you how to focus on your breathing and visualize a beautiful pasture and such. What the hell. I put it on and try to concentrate on what the guy is telling me to do. His voice is barely above a whisper, and there is the sound of gentle waves in the background. I think it is actually working, and I am feeling more relaxed. It helps take some of the chatter in my head away and sort of forces me to focus on something as straightforward and natural as my breathing pattern. I actually concentrate on feeling my muscles relax. My neck, my shoulders, my legs, my back. This is not bad. I may make a habit of this. I sort of break out of my trance and look at my phone where I am listening to the podcast. I've been doing this for 4 minutes, and the podcast is

22 minutes long. My first thought is that I can't do this for 22 minutes, I have too many other things to do. Besides, I am laying down, and if I try to do this for that long, I'll probably fall asleep. I put the phone down and try to get back into it, but I only make it to 11 minutes. I'll try to do more tomorrow. Little changes. I think they are good, and if I make it through this ordeal alive, I want to make them permanent. I want to live a more serene life. Less aggressive. Quieter. Is that weird? I don't think so. I don't think I am alone in feeling this way. The world has gotten so crazy, I think I'd be better off if I could tune it out completely sometimes. Quiet music. Meditation. Hey, it's a start.

October 18, 2012

Today is October 18th, and it's been 10 days since I started writing this. It sure seems longer. Now that I have come to grips with this I want to get it over with. But waiting is now the name of the game. Wait to get doctors' appointments, wait to see the doctor, and wait for results. Admittedly, I am not a patient person by nature, so maybe that is something else I need to work on.

Right now I just want things to go faster. Last week I had to get the MRI which was also a fiasco. The first appointment was at 8:30 at night and I couldn't eat all day. Between my acute needle phobia and not eating, I experienced a physical and mental breakdown when the otherwise friendly nurse said that my vein collapsed, and they couldn't get the IV into my arm. No MRI that night.

I had to wait for another MRI appointment, which happened to be today. With the help of a strong dose of Valium and a highly competent nurse, the MRI is over. The results are floating around in the universe of the unknown while I (you guessed it) wait.

I've gotten a second opinion from the guy who is supposed to be the second best surgeon for my type of cancer, and he sees it about the same way as the first guy. His surgical method is a bit more radical, and he wants to slice my entire belly open all the way down to my happy place. That doesn't sound too good so Dr. Matthews is still my first choice. He's going to look at the results of my MRI to figure out more precisely where this unwelcomed visitor is inside my body. I'm praying that the results of the MRI will not identify something new that we weren't expecting.

I guess I am going to need to find ways to deal with the uncertainty and lack of closure. If I sound more negative writing this, I suppose I am. No matter how hard I try, and I do, the gravity of having this disease takes its toll. It seems that every time I get good news, I can't help feeling like the next shoe is going to drop at any minute. Maybe it's the waiting, maybe it's just my nature, or maybe it's a premonition. I'm trying as hard as I can to keep my mind off it by working hard, talking through it with my loved ones and telling myself things are going to be ok.

I've got one more surgeon to see here in town and then I am going to figure out where the most prominent surgeon for colorectal cancer is in the world, and I am going to find a way to get in front of him or her. I've always heard that you should get a second opinion which I have. Maybe I'm more skeptical than most, and I need a third, fourth and fifth opinion. Whatever. It's my life on the line so I really don't give a shit if people think its overkill. If the top docs all tell me the same thing, I will feel more confident that it is the truth, and I will know what's coming. Gee wiz I actually feel more positive just writing this.

In other news, Russ spent a few days with me after our visit with Dr. Matthews, making me laugh and telling me everything was going to be ok. He made me get a manicure. That'll take your mind off of what ails you. As I sat there feeling awkward, I could only hope the petite little Vietnamese lady didn't cut my finger because it would hurt. A little nip of the skin on my finger, that's what I was worried about. I guess pain is a relative thing. In the very near future, I am going to have some guy slicing into my midsection, digging in up to his elbow and carving out pieces of my internal organs. You think about weird things when you have cancer. Anyway, the time with Russ was fun and very good for me.

Nancy is doing a great job of budgeting the cash we had saved for a trip to Italy. The doc I saw last week said I could still go and schedule the surgery for when I get back, but we decided that fun and cancer tend not to reside in the same place. Italy will have to wait. I sure hope I get to see it again. I love Italy so much, and there is so much of it I have yet to experience. If I get through this, I will cherish my time there more than ever.

October 19th, 2012

When my phone rang, I anxiously looked at the caller ID. Dr. Matthews. I didn't realize that a person could experience such a wide range of intense emotions in the span of about 3 seconds. Panic. What is he calling me about? Is this his office and am I going to hear the voice of one of his staff members when I pick up or is HE actually calling me? If it is him, there must be something wrong. Or maybe it's good news? Nah, they don't call with good news. They make you call them for that. Maybe I should just let it go to voice mail. That way I can gather myself and get prepared for the news. But they aren't going to leave any kind of news on a voice mail message, they are going to want to break it to me directly. Ok, I'll suck it up and answer. I can handle it. I have to face reality, and this call is about reality.

"Dan Colachicco," my standard answer when I pick up unless it is a family member. It's Dr. Matthews. His voice, and as usual, I can't tell if he sounds worried or upbeat. One thing I do like about this guy is that he gets right to it. No chitty chatty bullshit.

"We got the MRI images back, and everything looks the way we expected. There's no reason why we can't perform the surgery as I described it. I just wanted to call you personally to let you know because I know you're a worry-wart". If that is an insult, I'll take it. Another piece of apparent good news. So why do I still feel apprehensive? I am beginning to wonder if I even know how I actually feel about anything anymore. It is an overused metaphor, but my emotions are on a minute by minute roller coaster. I thank the good doctor and proceed to tell Nan what he said. She delivers her usual encouraging words with a smile and a hug, but I can also hear the relief in her voice. She acts like she knew it all along, but there is no doubt that she feels some of the same uncertainty that I am overwhelmed with. We both comment on how cool it is that the surgeon picked up the phone and actually called me himself instead of having one of his nurses or other staff members call. That is a good sign, and I'll remember it when I make my final decision on who to have do the surgery. So far, I'm pretty sure he's the guy.

I'm in this constant conversation with myself telling myself that everything indicates that I am going to get through this. Think positive. Negative thoughts aren't healthy. I am committed to being a healthier person both physically and mentally. Damn, though….it is hard work. The pictures of the tumor and the harsh delivery of the bad news from Dr. Weinstein still ring in my head, and there is no way to let it go. Think happy thoughts. Push the negative away. These are commands that I will deliver to myself daily for quite some time to come.

October 21, 2012

Today I am going to "get my affairs in order." I am hoping for the best, but to be smart about it I have to be prepared for the worst. Not getting life insurance which would have been so easy to do, is going to have me kicking myself in the pants for the rest of my life, however long that is. My needle phobia made me procrastinate pretty much forever and once I finally got it done, it was too late.

I got diagnosed a few weeks later and became "uninsurable." I would have so much more peace of mind if my family would not have to worry about money with me out of the picture, but I blew that. Not that I have been a great provider lately anyway. We are still struggling financially, and I guess we don't have that much in the way of assets that I need to address, but still, I want everything set up so that Nan won't have to deal with it if I am out of the picture. I decide I have to write down all of our accounts, how everything is titled, who we owe money to, and I need to tell Nan that we have a potentially valuable asset in the computer software I had developed. I need a business person whom I can trust to make sure that everything is taken care of in the event of my demise so I choose my long-time accountant and partner Mike. Mike is a guy that I trust beyond reproach. He knows the tax code inside and out and has always been there for me. He's never given me a bill. Ever. The only reason he has never given me a bill is because he is my friend. He is the most trustworthy individual I know, and I will write everything up and take everything to him. He will make sure that Nan doesn't have to deal with anything or anyone that she isn't comfortable dealing with, and he will protect her from anyone trying to take advantage of her.

I haven't told Mike about my colon cancer yet, and that is going to be a tough conversation. He just lost his wife of 30 years to cancer a few months ago. What the hell is it with this disease? I wonder how many people died of cancer 200 years ago? Maybe they couldn't diagnose it as easily. So people would get cancer, but doctors didn't know what it was.

I wonder if the reason cancer is so prevalent now is because of all the crap we put in our food and all of the environmental stuff we are exposed to every day? It just seems like you can't meet anyone who hasn't lost a friend or loved one to this fucking disease. And now I have it. I have to shake off these thoughts and get this stuff down on paper. That isn't easy because the very premise of writing this is the assumption that I am going to die soon.

It is hard to stay positive and think about a long future when you are writing about how things should be dealt with after you are dead. Still, writing it certainly doesn't mean that I am definitely going to die, it is just a smart way to prepare in the event it happens. I know it is going to happen eventually, and I know that this would be a smart thing to do even if I hadn't been diagnosed with this disease. I hope I think of everything so that it is easy for Mike to understand. I will go over it with Nan and tell her the plan so that in the worst case scenario all she has to do is contact Mike and he will take care of everything. I block the event that will trigger the need for this out of my mind so that I can concentrate on getting everything down on paper.

October 22, 2012

I am meeting with Mike this morning to tell him what's going on and deliver the package of information I put together last night. Mike is an interesting cat. He had some sort of bet with his son, the details of which I don't remember, but the result was that he stopped cutting his hair. So Mike has shoulder length pure white hair that he does not spend a lot, scratch that, he spends absolutely no time styling. This is one of the things I like most about Mike. He is the genuine article. What you see is what you get, and he doesn't need to impress anybody. He is comfortable in his own skin, and he directs his life the way he wants it to go. He is also one of the most brilliant minds that I know when it comes to taxation and business in general. He is creative yet practical and very conservative. He treats his clients' money like it is his money and protects it vigorously.

We start with the usual small talk, but I can't really fake all of the burden I am carrying so I get right to it. I tell him that I recently got some bad news health wise and just blurt out that I found out that I have colon cancer.

I keep talking, but Mike's reaction tells me that I just hit him on the head with a ball peen hammer. His hands move up to cover his mouth, and his face starts to contort. I continue on with telling him why I am there and about the information I put together last night, but I begin to lose my train of thought when I see the tears.

My good friend, my confidant, and my business partner is shedding tears for me. His entire body becomes taught, and he is making no effort to hide his emotional reaction. I wasn't expecting this. I don't know exactly what I was expecting and was concerned that he was going to relate my cancer to the loss of his wife. But I was not expecting a breakdown. He isn't saying anything but acknowledging the things I am describing from the document with nods of his head. I finally tell him I am sorry that I upset him, and I am very optimistic. I feel that the prognosis is good, and I have every intention of beating this and not having a need for him to refer to these documents anytime soon.

I then feel that I need to tell him that the reason I am giving all of this to him is that he is the single most trustworthy person I know. With that, there are more tears and a forced "thank you" through the raw emotion. I am feeling both flattered and sad. I am touched that Mike cares enough for me that learning of my diagnosis causes such a reaction, but I feel bad that I upset him. I am sure he is thinking of the horrible stuff he went through over the past year dealing with his wife's cancer. He probably knows more about what I am about to go through than I do. Hopefully, there is a better outcome for me in the future than what he experienced. Hopefully, we will be able to look back on this and talk about how I "beat it."

He takes the papers without really looking at them too much. He put them in his desk drawer, presumably to review later. I have a feeling of comfort knowing that I just did a smart thing for my family. My sons are grown, but if the worst happens they will not be emotionally prepared to deal with this stuff, and they are young. A seasoned advisor like Mike whom I am entrusting with my family is a gift that not many other people have the luxury of. I give Mike a half-hearted "man hug" and tell him everything is going to be alright. I can feel myself smiling, and it is sincere.

October 28, 2012

I found this Doc at Johns Hopkins in Baltimore. He's supposed to be the best surgeon for colorectal cancer in the US. We've decided to spring for a road trip and get one last opinion from this supposed genius. That will be the fourth surgeon I've seen, and then it will be time to pull the trigger.

I am more anxious every day. I sometimes wish I could completely ditch the surgery and let fate take its course, and other times want to schedule the damn surgery for the next day so I can get on with my life. Then I think about my beautiful wife and my precious sons. I envision my boys asking their mom, "Why didn't dad do anything to try and get better? Why did he choose to do nothing and leave us behind without him?" Doing nothing is a coward's way, and I would like to think that cowardice is not part of my DNA. For all intents and purposes, doing nothing is probably committing suicide and I sure as hell don't want to do that. I may not win, but I am not going to go down without a fight.

We are set to fly to Baltimore on November 12th and go to the world famous Johns Hopkins to meet this big shot. I am also going to get a little family time with my cousins and try to enjoy the travel. Hopefully the news I get from Dr. Big Shot is consistent with what I am hearing from the other guys and I'll feel confident enough that I can get this show on the road.

Nobody will be able to say that I didn't gather as much decision-making data as possible before giving the green light.

Thinking about it I am actually getting kind of excited about making the trip. I love that area, and the cool weather will be nice. I love to travel and hopefully if I have a positive outcome it is something I will look forward to for a few more years. It's weird to think of things in those terms. Everything that pops into my mind is tainted with the possibility of death and finality. I want to look to the future, but I then realize, I may not have much of a future left. This is my new reality, and in an ironic way, I think it is a good thing. It makes me much more appreciative of every day… hell, of every second of every day. If I get my "second chance" I will cherish the things I value in life more than I ever have before. I've taken so much for granted. I am so fortunate and will be thankful every day for the rest of my life, however long that may be. The things that have always seemed like "problems" are really so small and insignificant. It almost makes me laugh. Never again will I let silly little challenges overwhelm me. Gratitude is my new attitude.

November 7th, 2012

I am actually feeling pretty good right now. Work is keeping my mind off of things, and my new-found healthy diet seems to be kicking in. I'm losing weight and feeling energized. I sure don't feel like I have a killer disease. Of course, the symptoms are still there which send me that not so subtle reminder every time I see them, but there is no pain.

I used to make fun of Russ for eating the stuff that I now eat every day. I used to joke that he was ingesting "liquid weeds" because the thing he would make would be a green leaf infused concoction. Now he has me drinking them, and I have to say, I'm actually starting to enjoy it. The shakes for breakfast look awful but are pretty tasty, and I like knowing that I am putting nutritious food into my old body.

I can't help but wonder if I have colon cancer because of all the crap I've eaten over the years. Was I slowly killing myself with what I was eating? Oh yeah, I talked a lot about being healthy, but in reality, I made plenty of poor dietary choices. I typically would eat for pleasure and gave no consideration to the long-term effects of digesting unhealthy foods. I think healthy eating is a relative thing. There are plenty of people who are obese and have diets that make me look like an over-the-top health food nut. They don't have colon cancer, and maybe they never will.

Eating healthy is a decision that I make before every meal. It's a choice I have to make every time I decide on a restaurant to go to or what to say when Nan asks me what to make for dinner. I am going to get much more serious about this.

One good thing about the internet is it puts insane amounts of information at your fingertips so I am going to study nutrition like an animal and if I get past this damn surgery I will use food to heal my body and keep it in the best shape it can be for as long as possible.

I want to live, and I want to live without pain. I want to live without fear that something I eat will bring my cancer back. Maybe I'll even try to find a nutritionist to help me if I get through all of this. I am thinking about how good I feel right now knowing all of the nutritious stuff I've eaten so far today, and I can't help but believe that the two are related. I want to feel this good all the time. I also believe that eating right and working out every day leading up to this surgery can only be good for me. Huh. Positive thoughts. I wonder if the diet and exercise have anything to do with positive thinking. I choose to believe that they do so I am going to be really diligent about keeping up with both from now on. Whatever "now on" turns out to be.

November 14th, 2012

Johns Hopkins was most definitely not what I expected. I get that it is a world renowned hospital and that the doctors are highly sought after, but I had no idea it was such a circus. Just trying to park caused almost unbearable stress. The building is almost like an enclosed stadium, and they have this elaborate system for "checking you in." There are hundreds of people everywhere.

For the most part, you can tell the ones that are sick and the ones who are caring for them. I look at them, and I feel anxious. Everyone looks nervous and in some sort of distress. I know who the patients are. I'm one of them.

I see the nervousness in Nan's face, and I see that she is concerned about my anxiety. She knows me better than anyone so there is no sense in trying to hide it. That just makes it worse. I don't want her to have to go through this. Still, I am glad to have her by my side, and the support means so much.

As I play the never ending waiting game, Johns Hopkins style, I start to think about these people around me. Some of them are here because they got bad news like me. I'm sure some of them are here not knowing what the news will be today. Undoubtedly, some will leave with bad news. Some of these folks are going to get the Dr. Weinstein treatment that I got a month or so ago. They are going to see those ugly pictures, and their lives are going to seem devastated in a single moment. I feel so sorry for them. The nervous family members who are here with them now are going to have a lot to deal with as well. The memory of getting that news is still so fresh and stinging in my mind that even as I write about it now, my stomach hurts. I wonder which of these people is going to start that painful journey today. It makes me sad and even more anxious. I want to get out of here. And then I hear my name called. Here we go....

I can't figure out the logic in moving you from one waiting area to another. Yeah, they do a little something like take your weight and ask you a few questions to make you feel like there is an actual reason why they moved you from one waiting area to another, but I think it's all a psychological game. They have to keep you moving because if they make you wait in one place the whole time you'll get pissed. They must think a change of scenery will help to deflect that. It doesn't work with me. I know the game, and I don't like it. There are more people in this little waiting area than there are chairs. It's maddening, and I really think that this was a bad idea. I can't believe that this is the world renowned Johns Hopkins. It looks like a cattle call. I'm already 90 minutes past my appointment time which makes me nuts. Why have a freaking appointment at a particular time if they are going to miss it by a mile? This room is as bad as the first waiting area with all of the sad and worried faces. I am fighting the urge to say “screw it” and leave. I had to work so hard to get this appointment, and this guy is supposed to be the best of the best. I have to stay, but I am almost getting physically ill from the anxiety.

Finally, I hear the nurse call my name, albeit a ridiculously bad pronunciation.

Down a long white sterile hallway, we go to the exam room. There must be a hundred exam rooms on this floor. I am wondering which one this big shot surgeon is in and how long it will be before he finds his way to mine. The PA asks me more questions and confirms receiving the disc with the CT scan and other reports I sent them. Two hours past my appointment time now. Nan is trying to calm me down like she always does, but I can’t control showing my frustration. I shouldn’t be so rude to her when I get like this and I try to suppress my desire to lash out. We start exploring what if scenarios. What if he wants to give me a full exam? Blood tests? Send me to a lab? I don’t want any of that crap right now. I just want to talk to the guy and as quickly and concisely as possible have him tell me that he agrees or disagrees with Dr. Matthews’s assessment of my condition. I’m going to tell him that as soon as he walks in the door.

Fifteen minutes later there is a knock immediately followed by the entry of the Doc and his assistant. He's got my file and gives us a friendly but professional greeting. All of my apprehension seems to melt away within seconds after meeting him, and he starts right in on his opinion about what he sees. He agrees with everything Dr. Matthews said. He is optimistic and pretty much confirms everything I've heard up to this point. I take advantage of the time with him to ask my usual litany of questions about recovery, the possibility of a "bag," long term effects, etc.

He gave me the usual non-committal answers which equate to "anything and everything are possible" but he also brings up a word I had yet to hear. He said that sometimes this type of surgery results in "reverse ejaculation." Huh? That is possible? He then explains what it is to me and for the most part, it is precisely what the name describes. I cannot help but ask him to elaborate which he gladly does. Of course, it leads to a much needed few moments of levity.

After all of the grueling wait time, the anxiety, and the depression I have had for the past several hours, I embrace this opportunity to just laugh at this very quirky possible after effect of my colorectal cancer surgery. I look at Nan, and she knows that I am going to ride the shit out of this one when we leave. It is almost like a pressure release to talk about this, no pun intended.

My mind is focused on what the doc is saying, but at the same time, I know I have my validation. I know this is the end of the guess work, and it is time to move this process to the next stage. I am feeling more confident that I have a handle on this disease, and there is a consensus from really well-trained professionals on what needs to be done to make me better. I'm cutting loose the negative feelings I have built up over the past few hours and just getting thankful for the outcome. Having said that, I am sooooo ready to get the hell out of this building. We have dinner planned with the cousins, and I turn my focus to family time.

November 15th. 2012

We have breakfast at the hotel when my cell phone rings and the caller ID says it is Dr. Matthews. I can't help but get anxious every time I see that on my phone. I have to get over all of the pre-judging about what he is calling about. I'm probably going to get a zillion calls from his office over the next few months. Still, I can't help but think about the day he called me personally, and I have to wonder whose voice I am going to hear this time.

It's Dolly, the nurse who schedules the surgery. Scheduling operations and procedures are her functions at Dr. Matthews's office. I can't imagine how many calls like this she makes every day. The guy does schedule surgeries once a week and emergency surgeries as they come up. So the call for her is routine. For me? Not so much. The anxiety is kicking in again, but I know this is where we go next. Time is not on my side, and the sooner I can get this out of the way, the better. She rattles off a couple of dates, but we decide on November 27th. The Tuesday after Thanksgiving. He also wants me to have the other polyps removed before the surgery so we are scheduling another colonoscopy for this Tuesday, the 20th. Whoa. We are zooming now.

November 20th, 2012

Interesting day today. I am trying to resolve my phobia of needles, but it still freaks me out. I've had a couple now, and it never seems to be as bad as I make it out to be in my mind. Still, as I prepare for the colonoscopy this morning, I ask the anesthesiologist if he could give me something like a valium for the anxiety before sticking me. Really nice guy, tells me that they have an easy solution which is that they can give me some of the ether before sticking me, and I probably won't even notice it. Awesome!! They roll my nervous ass back to the operating room. It is glaringly bright, and the machinery looks like it is capable of doing a lot more than fishing a cable up my butt. The friendly anesthesiologist guy who, for now, is my best friend makes some funny comment about the ether as they put it over my nose. I think I laughed, but I am not sure. Three seconds later, I was out. Needle? What needle?

When I feel myself waking up, I open my eyes to see a nice little private room, dimly lit. No scary machinery. No people. I have a nice warm blanket covering me up to my chin. I take an assessment of my condition. Pain? Zero. I feel pretty good, and it's nice to know that this part of the process is over. But now I am anxious to know what he found when he went in there. Even though I haven't really been too worried about this leftover polyp, I'd like to hear directly from the doc that it's all good. I find myself hungry for good news at every stage of the game. The fear is always going to be there, but the good news along the way gives me those tinges of relief that I have come to really appreciate.

I'm actually coming out of the fog now, and I can hear voices. Dr. Matthews has a distinctive voice. It kind of sounds like a guy you'd have beers with. It is raspy, like a man who has been talking too loud over too long or maybe smoking for 20 years. I hear him in the hallway outside my little room. I also hear Nancy's voice. They are talking, and I strain to listen to what they are saying. Is he giving her bad news? My head is totally clear now as I strain to hear every word.

"What the hell are we going to do about this needle problem? I'm really concerned about it." Dr. Matthews is concerned about the needle problem? Does he mean my phobia? We solved that. A little ether and whoosh, I'm good for whatever steely jab you want to hit me with. What is the problem?

"I mean we do that for little kids who are screaming and crying. We didn't set it up to do the anesthesia this way. Dr. London took it upon himself to handle it, but he can't expect this every time he's got to get poked. This is a real problem." Did he compare me to a little kid screaming and crying? He's telling my wife this? Sounds like a little bit of an overreaction to me. Ok, so I don't like needles, and I get a little freaked out, but c'mon doc. Is this the most pressing thing you have to talk to my wife about? Come and talk to me. I'm getting a little pissed, and I'd like to talk through this monumental problem you are discussing with my wife.

"HEY. DR. MATTHEWS STOP TALKING TO HER. COME IN HERE AND TALK TO ME," I say. I'm noticeably yelling at this point. Finally, I see him turn toward my room. "Stop busting my fucking balls about the needles," I say in a less than respectful manner. What the hell. He'll think I am still feeling the effects of the anesthesia, and I'll be forgiven.

"What's the fucking problem? I don't like needles, but I'm dealing with it." I realize that I am opening up a confrontation with the guy who is going to cut into my body next week. Maybe this is a bad idea.

He then gives me the same speech he just gave Nancy about the anesthesiologist doing me such a big favor since they usually only do the ether thing for little kids. I think he is busting my balls.

"…I mean you're going to have to get stuck like 500 times through this ordeal, and I am worried about it. Am I going to have to put a port in you?" He is trying to sound sincerely concerned, but I can't help but think he is egging me on.

“Doc. I’ll deal with the needles. What do you mean by putting a ‘port’ in me?”

“We insert a port in your chest, and all the needles go through the IV. We can even draw blood when we need to. I think we’ll have to put a port in and then you won’t have to deal with the needles in the hospital”.

“Ok, fine. Whatever. But quit busting on me about the fucking needles. It’s not that big a deal. What happened with the colonoscopy? Is everything ok?” “Yeah, we took the rest of them out. You’re all set. See you next week.” And with that, he pats me on the knee and heads for the door.

The last time I had a colonoscopy Nan and I talked about going to breakfast afterward, something we seldom do unless we are on vacation. Since the news was good today and we are really trying to gear up for my big surgery, we decide to go to breakfast. We always have so much to talk about.

I continually remind myself how grateful I am to have a life partner that is on the same page with me. There is no one on the planet I’d rather be with at any given moment. So needless to say, I’m really looking forward to breakfast. My outlook is more confident, and I have put most of my fear on the back burner now. At this point, I just want to be with my family, have a nice Thanksgiving, and get this shit over with. I am expecting to be up and around by Christmas and back to work by New Years. Positivity. How refreshing.

Most of our breakfast talk revolves around my little yelling match with Dr. Matthews. Nan has concerns that I shouldn't have spoken to him that way, but I think he can handle it. I still believe he got some twisted pleasure out of teasing me about the needles. Either that or maybe it was a strategy to get me to overcome my fear. The guy is definitely smart enough to pull off some sort of psych thing like that, but I just don't know. Oh well, we have a good laugh about it, and I tell Nan that I am not afraid of needles anymore. Not sure that's true, but if I say it enough maybe it will start to become so.

Thanksgiving Day, 2012

I manage to have the day off even though most of my colleagues are working today. Part of me wishes that I was working too. Being around my friends at work and keeping busy takes my mind off my upcoming surgery. Some people I work with know about my cancer, but many of them don't.

I have done a great job of maintaining a positive, upbeat attitude at work, so I think my colleagues who do know are impressed. I'm glad I'm not getting a lot of the usual "you're in our thoughts and prayers" stuff from them. We laugh and bust on the customers and the craziness of the business. I like the people I work with, and I have to remind myself how blessed I am to work for a company that is so supportive and provides me such great benefits. Man, without the benefits I am not really sure what I would be doing right now. I'm sure I am still going to have a boatload of bills, but the cost of this whole ordeal is beyond my comprehension. Hell, I've gotten 4 opinions from 4 pretty well-renowned surgeons, I've had tons of tests, 2 colonoscopies, MRI, CT Scan…. I'm surprised I don't glow in the freaking dark. But I've only come out of pocket a few bucks. I sure am thankful for this job with this great company right now. They even have an awesome Case Manager, Dawn, who calls me to talk to me about my condition. She is assigned as an advocate that acts on my behalf to expedite appointment scheduling or getting my questions answered. It's included in my insurance benefits. Kind of cool.

Gratitude seems to come to me so much easier since I found out I am ill. I think about the things I am grateful for often. I like that. It feels good. I plan on keeping this "attitude of gratitude" for the rest of my days. I take a moment to soak in the fact that today is Thanksgiving, and again, I think about how much I have to be thankful for. It's a long list.

Nan is running around already trying to get this massive feast together like she does every year. The kids will be here, and Billy's bringing his girlfriend. I want it to be a chill day, and I want us all to just hang and relax. I think that is how this day is supposed to be. Thanksgiving dinner is a lot of work for Nan, and that bothers me. I can't tell whether she actually likes doing it or she feels obligated. I think she would agree that it gets her unnecessarily frazzled. The stress kind of permeates the air and it doesn't feel very festive, at least not to my way of thinking. Sure, once we all sit down at the table and start yapping and laughing everything is great, but all of the angst that goes into getting to that point makes me wonder if it's really worth it. I am happy for this day, but can't help wondering if this is the last Thanksgiving that all of us will be sitting around this table. Holidays conjure up these thoughts.

There is a shadow of finality that is ever present with almost everything I do. Just facing the fact that there is an end to life as we know it is sobering, but thinking that the end may be within sight hangs like a cloud over me and sneaks into my thoughts at random, stealing my happy moments. I'm having one of those moments now. Being together like this emphasizes how much I have to lose.

I have all of my family with me today, and I need to be infinitely grateful for that. If it is one of the last times, I'd better make the most of it. I want to make this day as enjoyable for Nan as I want it to be for me so I will go over the top and out of my way to help her so she isn't so stressed out. That will make me happy, and I want to grasp for every moment of happiness I can find. I will try to get the boys to help too but not to the extent that I am badgering or causing friction. This is supposed to be a day to give thanks, and I want to keep my focus on that. I have a lot to be thankful for.... A helluva lot!

If this all ends up not going my way, I want to remember this moment when I realized that I have had a really great life that most people don't get to experience. I have an abundance of love from my wife and my children. I had wonderful parents who raised me to be a solid human being with good character. I've traveled to amazing places, I've experienced amazing things.

I have created a legacy by bringing two awesome sons into the world whom I love unconditionally and who make me proud every single day. I am thankful and will remain so no matter what the outcome of this ordeal ends up being. I hope it will be many years before I look back on my life and reflect, but if God does not afford me that opportunity I can do it now and know that I have been blessed with an amazing life.

Today is Thanksgiving, and it means a lot more to me right now than turkey and football. Every Thanksgiving that I am given the gift of in the future will make me remember these things that I am so grateful for today. Really I want to look at every day as Thanksgiving and I will.

Thinking through this really helps me develop a positive attitude for the day. This time next week I will be in a hospital bed recovering. Hoping that everything was successful. Hoping I get my second chance. Hoping I will get better and have the opportunity to be blessed with more Thanksgivings in the future. Hoping I get to visit Italy again. For right now, I am "in the moment" and enjoying this beautiful day with my family.

November 23, 2012

Black Friday. Walking out of work today I am starting to feel the weight of reality set in. I think about only having 2 more days of work and then beginning this ordeal that I have thought about constantly for the past month and a half. It seems like years since my diagnosis. Another time. Like it happened to another person. In a way, it did because I really am not the same person that I was before October 4th. I am much humbler and probably a bit meeker. But I still have my moments of courage, and I am ready to fight for my life. I have a lot of good data that indicates my prognosis is good, so I try hard to cling to that.

I am skeptical by nature so fighting that off requires a seemingly constant argument inside my head. Part of me saying "I got this" and part of me waiting for the inevitable bad news to come. Somebody read a test wrong. They found something new. It's worse than they initially thought. Luckily that has not happened yet, but it hangs over my thoughts like a rain cloud waiting to ruin my day at the beach.

Yesterday was great, and it was a sort of milestone in my countdown to Tuesday. Up until that time, I wouldn't even talk about the surgery. The surgery was "after Thanksgiving." Now it is after Thanksgiving, and I feel like I am on a slippery slope speeding toward Tuesday.

I still wish it would all go away, but I like to pride myself as a realist. I know that while very unpleasant, this is my opportunity to beat cancer. I guess that if I do, I'll be one of those Cancer Survivor people that I see in the commercials and on billboards. I'd like to have that moniker. I like the survivor idea. It feels like a victory.

I have a long drive home, listening to my nifty new soft jazz station. I keep the volume down and concentrate on trying to enjoy the piano. I am focusing on my breathing, but I can't keep the thoughts out of my head. Two more days of work then I am off for 6 weeks. Is it really going to take me that long to recover?

I am nervous but excited to get this over with. I think I do a pretty good job of being casual and nonchalant about the upcoming surgery, even though I have all this pent up emotion inside of me.

I start thinking about having to get another blood test and hence another needle stick on Monday. It's the prep before the surgery. I hate needles. Then I get stuck again on Tuesday. After my little blow up with Dr. Matthews about the needles, I am just going to suck it up and show him it isn't going to bother me. That should be the biggest thing I have to worry about through all of this. I'll keep telling myself that.

November 25th, 2012

I pretty much spent the whole morning having coffee with Nancy and talking through a lot of philosophical stuff. It is a beautiful day, and I appreciate beautiful days more than I used to. It's funny how something like this increases your awareness of things that you used to take for granted. I went outside just as the sun was starting to come up this morning and looked at the stars. I don't know how long I stood there in my pajamas staring at the sky, but I really enjoyed seeing all of the stars in the sky, fading as the light turned the few clouds there were beautiful shades of pink and orange. I wonder if this higher level of awareness will continue if everything turns out ok with the surgery? Or will life just take over? I make the commitment to appreciate these simple things more often if everything goes well and I make it through this.

Coffee talk consists of the practicality that we need in preparing for Tuesday and a lot of reflection about the strength of our relationship, the adversity we have overcome, and the life we will have after surgery. My wife gives me unconditional support and love, and that is something I value and treasure. She makes me *want* to get better.

We talk for about 3 hours and then have breakfast when we should be having lunch. She heads off to take care of her mom, and I head up to Hallmark to get her an anniversary card since our anniversary is about a week after I have the surgery. I know that I probably won't be able to go out much after I get home, so I want to make sure I can give it to her no matter what. I usually try to find funny cards and avoid the "mushy" ones, but this year I want to find something a little more heartfelt. It just feels like I should.

My mind is pretty clear all things considered. I'm actually not even worried about getting the blood test "poke" tomorrow. How about that. It does seem like a long time since I was first diagnosed even though it has only been a month and a half. Lots of anticipation and now the time is almost here. I know I can't move past this until I have the surgery so I am resolved to make the best of it.

November 26th, 2012

I have to stay busy today. I've gone over all of my preparations in my mind and think I have covered everything so that I can be out of commission for a while. I have to go pick up paperwork at Dr. Matthews's office, go to the drug store and buy two freaking Fleet enemas, and then go to the hospital and do my pre-op stuff.

I can't help but be a little nervous now but not as bad as I thought. I actually like having a lot of things to do today. I hit the gym one last time this morning, and that felt good. I had that nice feeling of being able to take my time with no limits. I think about when I might be able to work out again, if ever. If I end up with a colostomy bag I sure as hell won't be slinging it around the weight room. That is not a very pleasant thought. Not gonna happen. I'll be back there, and it will be part of making me strong again. I read that vigorous exercise keeps your immune system functioning and helps ward off cancer cells. I need to tap into as much of that as I can.

I stop at CVS and find a "two pack" of enemas. There's this funny drawing on the side of the box that shows you how to give yourself the enema. I take a picture of it with my phone and send it to Russ with some crude comment. We score on that one for about 3 hours. I think it's true that humor is the best medicine.

I stop at Dr. Matthews's, and the papers I need for pre-op are waiting at the front desk. I see the nurses and staff, and they are going about their daily routine. I guess I sort of expected them to wish me well or show concern for what I am about to go through, but I am sure they have done this a zillion times before. I am just another patient. No expression from them good or bad.

My pre-op appointment is at 1:00 and I get there 10 minutes early. There are 25 people in the waiting room. On any given day I assume there are always 25 people sitting in this room getting ready to have a surgery of some kind the next day.

After about 20 minutes I hear my name (or some variable pronunciation of my name) called. I sit at the desk of a very cheery and chipper gal who has all of my paperwork in front of her, and she starts explaining everything. Tanisha is her name, and she actually makes me feel a bit more relaxed. I even crack a few jokes, and she laughs. Humor is a great defense mechanism. More questions of course and a reiteration of all of my precautions and instructions before surgery. *I got it.*

She tells me to go back and wait in the lobby again, and they will call me back shortly. Its needle time, and I am starting to feel the anxiety. As I look around the room, it doesn't get any better. The damn TV is blaring, and they are talking about people who are still trying to recover from Super Storm Sandy.

A woman is weeping and telling the reporter how she lost everything. Not very uplifting.

I watch people in the waiting room, and they look like zombies to me. Reading magazines, staring with their arms crossed, not a single smiling face in the room. I have no idea what each of them is here for, but I would bet that, like me, each of them would rather be somewhere other than here.

Tanisha continues to call names up to her desk and eventually an older lady comes out through a side door and barks out my name. She introduces herself as Vicki, and she doesn't seem quite as bubbly as my new friend Tanisha. Nevertheless, she escorts me through the door and into the lab.

Once through that door, the entire environment changes appearance. No soft lighting or colorful carpet here. Glaring white fluorescents and a white speckled, linoleum tiled floor. I think the color scheme is called "Ultimate Sterility." Vicki walks me up to a scale and says "let's get your weight." Not that I am overly sensitive about my weight, but it always bugs me how they document your weight with all your clothes and shoes on and your pockets full. I am a bit touchy about accuracy, and I just don't think my "body weight" shouldn't include the weight of my clothes, shoes, and cell phone. Regardless, if I asked them to weigh me naked, they would probably redirect me to the mental hospital.

"212 pounds," Vicki says.

"That's bullshit; I was 207 at home this morning," I tell her. She doesn't even look up at me. She just writes something on her clipboard full of papers. Whatever. At least I know the truth.

I am following behind Vicki without even attempting to make conversation. The hallway has separate corridors leading off to the right and left as we walk by. Most of the people I see are healthcare workers, and there are little workstations with people in white coats and blue scrubs. Some are writing, but the rapid clicking of computer keyboards can be heard coming from several different directions. I see the little seats that look like elementary school desks with the plain wooden table to rest your arm on. I guess that is where I am headed next so I tense up a bit.

Vicki takes a sharp left, and we are in one of the open "lab" areas with the same desk I think I sat in when I was in the 4th grade. There is a computer station, and Vicki plops herself down on a little back rolling stool. She is navigating the mouse and clicking as she is staring at the screen intently.

We then rehash that I am allergic to penicillin and strawberries, and she reconfirms that I haven't taken any aspirin or ibuprofen in the past 7 days. We go through the lengthy list of all the vitamins I am now taking, and she is typing as I am speaking. I half expect her to make a comment about all of the nutrients I am pumping my body with but she is very unceremonious. She is obviously not impressed.

After another couple dozen questions, she moves over to the rolling metal tray that has all of the "stuff" they use to take your blood. Rubber strap, alcohol, test tubes and of course the skin impaler, (aka syringe). A quick glance and then I look away.

"Just letting you know I am allergic to needles. I hope you'll be gentle".

She kind of smiles and tells me not to worry, she does about 20 of these a day, and she has been a nurse for 15 years.

Vicki has chosen my right arm because it has the best veins. My head immediately turns 30 degrees to the left. She wraps the tourniquet around my right bicep and tells me to make a fist. She is feeling around with her fingers and then I feel the cold rubbing of alcohol in the center of my forearm.

"Just a little pinch," she says and then I feel the needle go in.

I'd say a little more than a "pinch" but certainly tolerable. I try to let my body relax, and I am not moving a muscle. After a few seconds, I feel Vicki remove the needle and push a cotton ball down on the spot where she so skillfully poked me. Not a big deal. After each blood test, I have thought to myself, "why do I get so freaked out? This isn't that bad."

The relief of knowing that this one is over washes over my body. Despite what I know I am in for tomorrow, I am in a much better mood. I have more energy, and I am going to try to relax the rest of the day and just let the events unfold naturally. What else can I do? There is a certain amount of peace that comes with feeling this way. I am not over thinking it like I have been for the past couple of months. By this time tomorrow, that fucking tumor will be out of my body, and hopefully, I will be on the road to recovery. I head out the front door with a little bit of a bounce in my step. I think I will grab some lunch.

Surgery

November 27th, 2012

I slept. If someone had bet me on it, I would have sworn that there would be no real sleeping between November 26th and November 27$^{th.}$ I take that as a good sign, but now I realize that it is 4:30 a.m. and I need to give myself the first of 2 fleet enemas. Just what I want to do at 4:30 in the morning. I read the funny little cartoon that gives the instructions on how to administer the thing and try to follow it just like the hand-drawn picture on the package. There is nothing natural about this. This feels really weird, but the results turn out like they are supposed to (I assume). I have to wait 2 hours and do this again.

I lay in bed doing a major self-analysis of my feelings at this moment. Surprisingly, I am very matter of fact about what is going to happen today. I can't deny that I have some butterflies, but I am ready for this to be over, and this is the first step. I tell myself that by this time tomorrow I will be recovering in the hospital, and I won't have this tumor inside of me anymore. That can only be a good thing, right? I retrace everything I have done on my own behalf since October 4th when Dr. Weinstein threw that ugly picture onto my lap and curtly told me that I had cancer. I have been over the top thorough in making sure I had all of the data needed to make a smart decision. All of the news from all of the tests has been good, and all indications are that I can beat this. I pretty much know exactly what they are going to do to me. Everything feels complete to this point. That feels good and makes me feel confident. I realize that the thing in life that makes me feel anxious and uneasy is the unknown. I can't help it. I have to know all of the details. A friend of mine had a name for this type of thought process: Trust but Verify. I definitely buy into the verify part, and I question how really trusting I am. Do I trust Dr. Matthews? Do I have a choice at this moment? I do believe that I made the right decision in going with him. With all of the people I know who have a personal relationship with him, it's almost like it was meant to be.

I realize that anything can happen, but I have to believe that everything is going to be okay. Now, only a few hours from "going under the knife," I do believe it. I feel it. I have a lot more living to do, and I will recover from this. There is this sense of knowing in my mind, and it is a very peaceful feeling.

I am so at peace that I actually doze off again for a few minutes. I find this amazing knowing that I usually worry myself sick (literally) about stuff like this. At least I used to. In about 30 minutes I need to experience the thrill of a second enema. I think about Russ making fun of me and my enemas. It is an ongoing joke.

I think about my boys and how supportive they have both been since they heard the news. I will joke with them about the enema when I am out of the hospital. Both of my sons have simply told me that I am going to be okay. Both of them really believe it, and never have made me feel like they were worried that they might lose their dad. I probably didn't realize it to the extent that I should have when they were telling me, but I can feel the confidence in their voices as I lay here now. I am so proud of both of them, and I love being their dad. It sounds so cliché but kids truly do grow up in a flash. Every phase is so precious. I want more, and that means I have to live through this. The dad relationship has expanded to a "friend" relationship as they have grown older and I cherish my time with them. We've had so many amazing experiences, but there are so many more moments to look forward to, and I want to be there for all of them.

Lots of things are flooding my head right now. I am concerned about work, my postoperative recovery, and Christmas. How am I going to buy gifts for everybody?

The alarm on my phone starts playing maracas which mean it's time for my second enema. It goes a little easier than the first. I hear Nancy in the living room and see the kitchen light go on. "Did you sleep at all?" she asks. I tell her that surprisingly, I slept pretty well.

The enemas are out of the way, and I am ready to get this party started. Nancy actually seems more nervous than me. She asks me if I'm sure I did the enemas correctly, and verifies what time we need to be at the hospital. She says she doesn't understand why we have to be there so early. She tells me again that her friend Barbara is going to be there with her while I am in surgery, and expresses how good a friend she is.

I am in the shower nonchalantly answering each question and acknowledging her statements. Within twenty minutes I am dressed and ready to get going. I look around and wonder when I will be able to take a shower in this bathroom again. I wonder how the recovery will be once I get home. I have to shake this off and focus on today.

"We need to leave in 10 minutes," I tell Nan. We really don't need to leave for 20 minutes, and she probably knows that, but I want the extra time to make sure we aren't late. "I'll be ready in five," she says to my surprise.

Ten minutes later, we are heading out the door. I take one last look at my house knowing the next time I come through this door I will not be in as good a shape as I am now, but I will be without a cancerous tumor.

The drive to the hospital is pretty quiet. I am more nervous now and just sort of staring out the window. Because Nan knows me so well, Nan doesn't try to make small talk. We pull up to the massive building and try to follow the rather complicated directions for parking the car. When you are arriving for surgery everything is specified, from where you park to how you dress.

As we walk toward the lighted entrance, I see people scurrying everywhere. Most of them are dressed in healthcare garb from scrubs to lab coats to those stiff looking cotton pants and shirt sets that the nurses now wear. I wonder how many people work here on any given day? Sickness is a big business.

There are wayfinding signs that point in different directions. Nan takes charge and guides me toward the "Admissions & Registration" department. It is an insanely long walk, but we finally arrive at a small glass enclosed room. I was expecting it to be a huge area like what we experienced at Johns Hopkins, but it was exactly the opposite.

There was no one at the desk and no one waiting. We thought for a moment that we were in the wrong place. Finally, a young lady appeared and took down all of our information. The usual questions ensued, and Nan fielded most of them. More paperwork and now it was time to just sit and wait as I had done countless times over the past couple of months.

The fear and nervousness intensify. Waiting does that to me. Nan puts her hand on my leg and gives me a little rub. She is holding up great and kind of half looking for her friend

Barbara. More people wander in with their bags of clothes and paperwork.

I wonder how long I am going to have to sit here before somebody comes out and gets this ordeal started. Fifteen minutes seemed like fifteen hours, but a short, stocky gentlemen in dull blue pants and shirt walks right up to me, holding a clipboard and greets me by name. He is very calm and tells me we are going to go back and get me prepared for surgery. He said that Nancy can come back right before they take me to surgery. Nancy tells me she loves me and that she will see me shortly.

For some reason, I am a little uneasy about the reason why they want to have Nan come back to see me just before they take me to the operating room. I tell myself I shouldn't feel that way, but I can't help thinking it is a bad thing. Like they are bringing her back to say her final goodbye to me. I know that isn't really the reason, but I can't shake the negative thought.

I am in full sensory overload mode now, even though the surroundings look generally familiar. Stark white floor, walls, and ceilings, steel equipment here and there, lots of healthcare workers running around.

We enter a large room that has a series of curtained off areas with hospital beds in them. My escort walks me into the very first one on the end. He has a big plastic bag that will hold my clothes and points to a gown and socks neatly laid out on the bed.

"You need to remove all of your clothes, including your underwear and put everything into this bag. You can put your shoes in this separate bag. Are you wearing any jewelry?" I hold up my left hand and show him my wedding ring.

"You'll need to take that off too. You can give it to your wife when she comes back. Just open the curtain a little when you are ready." And with that, he walks to the other side of the curtain, and I hear the high pitched sound of metal on metal as he slides the curtain closed.

I am alone in this cold little area getting naked. Even though nobody can see me, I feel like I just took a ding to my personal dignity. Before I take off my boxers, I sort of check the curtain to make sure there isn't a gap in the curtain which makes me chuckle to myself. I pick up this silly little hospital gown and quickly figure out the whole arms through the front, open back thing.

These gowns are intentionally designed to embarrass you, I am convinced of it. There is no such thing as "fit" when it comes to how it contours to your body. For the most part, "one size fits none."

The socks or booties have little rubber designs on the bottom and top so that you don't do a Tom Cruise dance and slide across the floor. I put them on and actually like the way they feel on my feet. I wonder if I will get to keep them? There are two strips of fabric hanging off the back of the gown, and I wonder if I should tie them. I decide to just go with holding them together so my bare ass isn't exposed to the world, not that anyone in this place would care.

I slide the curtain and leave about an 8-inch wide opening. I quickly maneuver back to the bed where I can position this ridiculous gown to cover all my vital areas. Through the opening in the curtain, I can see a bunch of people running around, and I hear beeps and hydraulic sounds from unidentifiable machines.

I wonder where Dr. Matthews is right now? I wonder when the guy will be back here and what he is going to do next? I wonder if I opened the curtain enough for him to see that I am "ready?" *AM* I ready?

The guy walks by my curtain opening, and we make eye contact. He sort of puts his hand up as if to say he'll be with me in a minute. He's a busy guy. It's clear that I don't have the only surgery on the books today.

I am laying there trying to determine if I am comfortable in this bed thing. The back is tilted so that my head is elevated and I realize it is actually pretty nice. I lay my head back and try to relax and even close my eyes. I focus on my breathing, hoping it will make me feel more at ease. But when I focus on my breathing I actually STOP breathing and then I have to take intentional breaths which screw up the whole concept. There is no sense in pretending that I am going to relax.

I hear the sound of my wife's voice, and see her walking toward the 8-inch doorway in my holding room curtain, followed by the nurse.

She's smiling as usual, and they appear to be having a spirited conversation as they walk toward me. He flings the curtain open, and Nancy takes a seat in the chair next to my new bed.

"How ya doing?" she asks.

"Well, I think I have executed the 'changing of the clothes' portion of this ordeal perfectly," I say. Nan tells me that Barbara arrived right after they took me back and that she was going to sit with her for as long as need be. That's awesome. I feel good knowing that Nancy will not be sitting in that depressing little waiting room down the hall by herself.

Nancy is closer to Barbara than to her own sisters. My two sister-in-laws haven't even offered to help take care of their own mother while Nancy takes care of me. We had to hire a private duty nurse to pick up the slack and Nancy plans to split her time between seeing me in the hospital and taking care of her mom every afternoon. I think about that and once again realize my wife is an angel, and she deserves better than all of this stress and worry. Her sisters should be ashamed of themselves.

I reluctantly take off my wedding band and hand it to her. “This doesn’t mean we’re not married anymore ya know,” I say trying to use humor to lighten the situation a bit. She takes the ring and puts it in her wallet.

It isn’t long before a bunch of nurses come in and once again start asking me questions. One of them puts two little plastic bracelets on my wrist and asks me to spell my name and tell her my date of birth. I think about screwing with her and telling her that I am Martin Luther King, but she doesn’t look like she has a great sense of humor. I ask about the anesthesiologist and she wants to know why. I tell her about the little trick they did for me last week with knocking me out before they stick me. Maybe they can do the same thing today I suggest. She says she will mention it to the anesthesiologist whom she says will be in to see me in a few minutes. This needle thing. I wish I could get over it.

I ask Nan if she has seen Dr. Matthews, and she says that someone told her that he has already done two surgeries this morning. That kind of blows my mind. I guess this is very routine for him, but that is hard for me to wrap my head around. Are all of these surgeries for cancer? Life and death? How the hell does anyone cope with the gravity of this situation as a day to day job? I realize that I am just another one of his patients, nothing special. But he has treated me like I am special. That is a good thing I tell myself.

A few more minutes pass and a tall guy in scrubs enter my curtained palace. He's got one of those blue "I do surgery" beanies on his head.

"I'm Dr. Grey, and I'll be administering the anesthesia today."

He looks pretty capable. Dr. Grey goes over some stuff on my chart and re-states that I am allergic to penicillin and strawberries. He asks me what happens to me when I eat strawberries. Is that because he is curious or is they planning to use strawberries at some point in my surgery? I think about cracking a joke and asking him that, but my reflex is to just answer.

"Well I haven't had any since I was about 10, but my recollection is that I break out in a rash or hives or something like that."

Dr. Grey barely looks up and says "What about with the penicillin?"

"Hives there too I think, but again I haven't had any of it since I was a kid."

He seems satisfied with those responses and continues writing stuff in the chart. He tells me that they will give me something before they take me back to help relax me and take the anxiety away.

I proceed to tell him the story of what the previous anesthesiologist did with the gas before the needle thing. He stares at me kind of funny.

"We can do that, but we won't be able to give you the medicine to relax you before we go back." I'm ok with that I tell him, and with that, he smiles and pats me on the knee. He smiles at Nancy and says that Dr. Matthews will be in to see us shortly.

Ok, got that out of the way. I wonder if Dr. Matthews is going to give me a hard time about getting the gas before the needle again? I really don't care at this point. I was ready for them to stick me beforehand but if this is easier and makes me worry less, why not?

Nancy is getting antsier than I am at this point and she asks me again if I have seen Dr. Matthews. No, I haven't. I probably sounded like I had a little bit of an edgy attitude and I immediately wished I had not answered that way. For whatever reason, we both get snippy in these stressful situations, and unfortunately, we play off of each other when that happens. The same thing happens in a positive way when we are happy and excited about something, but it is way more noticeable when we are stressing over something. I half whisper to her "sorry."

I've now been laying in this hospital bed or gurney or whatever it is for about 45 minutes. I've seen people that were already in the other curtain covered rooms when I came in, get wheeled off to have their surgery. Maybe I am becoming desensitized to seeing hospitalized people because watching them go by with the machines and tubes protruding from their bodies used to really bother me. Now I just wonder if them leaving puts me closer to being next.

Down the hall, to my left, I hear the familiar gravelly voice of Dr. Matthews talking with several other people. They sound like they are getting closer, and I only have a moment to question whether or not they are coming to see me. The curtain gets flung wide open with some force.

"Mr. Colachicco! Are we finally going to get this thing out of you? I swear I thought you were going to take forever to make a decision on this."

Despite the mildly antagonistic words, Dr. Matthews is grinning from ear to ear when he is speaking them. He is in his surgical scrubs from head to toe, but as usual, he looks unshaven and disheveled. He is surrounded by three females also dressed from head to toe in surgical scrubs. He introduces them one by one, but I immediately forget their names. There are a few seconds of harsh realization that this is now about to happen. Minutes away probably. I feel ready and try to re-focus on what they are saying.

“We’re going to get this thing out of you today, ok? I spoke with Dr. Grey, and he is going to give you some gas before the IV so no worries there.”

Good. He didn’t take a shot at me about the needle thing again.

“We’re putting a port in so after the surgery they can take blood and give you your meds through that, and you won’t have to get poked 15 times a day. Then we’ll set you up an appointment with Dr. Zach in the next few weeks ‘cause there is about a 90% chance you’re going to need chemo after the surgery.”

Whoa……WHAT WAS THAT? CHEMO? AS IN CHEMO – THERAPY? HAIR FALLING OUT, SICK, VOMITING, LISTLESSNESS, CHEMO FREAKING THERAPY?

“Chemo?” Nancy and I say it almost in unison.

“You never said anything to me about having to have chemo after the surgery doc.”

“Well you’re so nervous anyway I didn’t want to freak you out any more than you already were so I just didn’t bother to tell you, but in these cases, it's almost certain that you'll need some amount of chemo to make sure we got everything. Don't worry about that now, let's get this over with and then you can go talk to the oncologist."

And with that, he got up and started talking to the nurses who were huddled around him like players getting the play from the star quarterback.

I looked at Nancy, and she looked at me.

Chemo? I obviously know that Chemo is a treatment for cancer and I have cancer, but he never discussed anything related to needing chemo so I assumed it wasn't part of what I was going to experience. I just assumed that he would slice that little bastard out of me, sew me back together and I would heal. Why would he drop this bombshell on me minutes before going into surgery? Maybe it is a good thing. I sure as hell won't have time to dwell on it. I can't help but be a little pissed.

Dr. Matthews walks off briskly and two of the nurses he was with come up to my bed and pull the side rails up. They are talking, but I am not hearing much of what they are saying. I get the gist when Nancy bends over and squeezes my arm, kisses me on the head and tells me everything is going to be alright. They've told her to go back to the waiting area, and I feel the nurse's foot release the brakes on the wheels under the bed. Someone puts a warm blanket over my legs and the bed is starting to move.

There are four people rolling my bed toward the operating room. I am overcome by the feeling that I have no control over anything that happens to me at this point. Normally that would give me a not so mild panic attack, but right now I am totally ok with it. The time has come for this to happen and I really have no choice but to trust the doctors and nurses who will have my life in their skilled hands. Still, I can't fight off the negative thoughts. What if I go under the anesthesia, and something goes wrong. I never wake up. It happens. Not likely and I just don't believe that will happen to me. I am telling myself to relax, and I try to think of something funny to say.

"Take it easy over the speed bumps, I kinda have to pee," I said to no one in particular. I hear a giggle and a comment, but I can't quite make out what the nurse said. It doesn't matter. The lame attempt at humor was more for me than them. Humor has always been my strongest defense mechanism.

It seems like we are going a long way and just about the time I realize that we come to a halt. I am still in a hallway, and the nurses are disbursing away from me. There is a lot of waiting in healthcare. Another male nurse comes up from behind my head and rolls the gurney backward through a double swinging door. One look around, and there is no question that this is the operating room. It is brighter than a night game at Yankee Stadium, and there must be ten people in scrubs positioned around some very ominous looking equipment. There are some undistinguishable sounds coming from my left. Whooshing and beeping sounds. I see Dr. Gray, and he hovers over me. He has a surgical mask covering his face, but I can tell he is smiling. He doesn't say anything, but I can hear several other people talking. I don't see Dr. Matthews, but I think I hear his voice.

I feel a moment of panic. The power of the room, the people, and the equipment hit me, and I am afraid. The sooner they can put me out the better. I don't need to be seeing all of this stuff.

"I'm going to put this mask over your nose and mouth. It will smell something like plastic. It will relax you and then we will administer the anesthesia. You doing ok so far?" Dr. Gray asks.

I just nodded my head, and I am sure he could tell that I was not entirely truthful at that moment. He pats me on the shoulder and adjusts some tubing on the plastic mask. I feel another person rubbing alcohol on my right arm, and I see the plastic mask cupped in Dr. Gray's hand. He gently places it over my face and before I have an opportunity to take a breath,

I feel a sharp pinch in my right arm. I cringe, and for a second I feel angry.

"I thought the plan was that I was going to be out when you stuck me?" I wanted to say, but I didn't think I could speak with the mask over my face. Whatever. It's over now, and as usual, it wasn't so bad.

I decide to accelerate the process and take a deep breath. Yup, it smells like fresh plastic. Pungent and sweet. A tingling sensation comes across my face, and my eyes get heavy. I think I will take one more deep breath……. That is the last thing I remember before waking up in the recovery room.

I have no idea how long the surgery took. With all of my research and information gathering, one thing that I never really looked into was how long this whole thing would take. Over the next couple of days, I would really lose track of time which is unusual for me. I am a clock watcher. Time is something that I stay aware of and sometimes that is good and sometimes it drives me crazy.

I create too many expectations for the things I need to get done in the amount of time I have which often causes me to seem rushed. One of my few memories, when I woke up in the recovery room, was wondering what time it was. Hell, I didn't know what day it was. Being put out with anesthesia is not like getting a good night's sleep. It is like leaving the planet and returning sometime in the future. There are tubes in my nose. I feel them pressing against my upper lip and the side of my face. My eyes feel like they are covered over with film, but I am beginning to focus. I see my beautiful wife's face. She is talking, but I can't really make out what she is saying. Am I dreaming this or is it real? The rest of the surroundings start to enter my awareness, and I realize that all of this is real. I am waking up. My torso is propped up in the bed at about a 30-degree angle.

There is an older nurse behind my wife maneuvering her way toward a machine that is beeping. Why do all these machines beep and what do the beeps mean? There doesn't seem to be a lot of room for the nurse to maneuver behind Nancy and I wonder if they have put me in a really small room.

"Can you hear me? Danny?" I hear Nancy say. I try to nod my head, but I'm not really sure if I did or not.

"Everything went fine. You're in the recovery room."

This is the recovery room. The surgery is over. I didn't die. I don't have a tumor in me anymore. Nancy says everything went fine. What time is it? What difference does it make…I sure as hell am not going anywhere. Nan's words bring me a little further out of the fog, and I try to look around a little to see what's going on.

The recovery "room" is really just another curtained off space with my bed in it. I don't see the nurse anymore, just Nan. She is rubbing my hand asking me how I'm doing. I have no idea how I'm doing. Right now I am just facing the reality that the surgery is over, and I am starting the next phase.

I must be in pain. I try to focus on my body. I recall Dr. Matthews's messy drawing of where they were going to cut me open, and I try to focus on my abdomen. Does it hurt? Nada. No pain. I actually don't seem to feel anything down there. How is that possible?

I look to my left and see tubes extending from under my gown up toward a bag of fluids and that stupid beeping machine. I can't really tell where the tubes originate, but I am pretty sure their starting point is somewhere under my skin. That must hurt I tell myself, but I don't feel any pain.

I am groggy, but I come to the conclusion that I am actually quite comfortable. Even relaxed. Maybe this is going to be way easier than I thought! I try to smile and turn my hand over to hold Nancy's hand. She is my angel. Just the sight of her gives me hope and makes me feel happy. She makes me want to fight to get better as fast as I can so that she will be proud of me. We have a lot more in our collective bucket list, and I need to be healthy so that I can make those things happen.

I try my best to acknowledge her in some sort of a positive way… a smile or and a squeeze of her hand. I want to say something, but I'm not quite sure I can.

"I'm good" I manage to weakly say.

"Are you cold? They have warm blankets" she says. Without waiting for me to answer, she turns to the nurse who is just outside the opening of the curtains and tells her she wants one of those "toasty" blankets. A short moment later I feel the soft warmth of the blanket over my legs where just a sheet had been before. She takes such good care of me. I am so lucky. I wish I could just get out of this bed and give her a big hug.

"They are getting a room ready for you and Dr. Matthews should be here in a few minutes to talk to us. I talked to him before they brought you in here and he said the surgery went well," she says.

The last time I heard his voice, he dropped the bomb on me that I would probably need chemo. It kind of pisses me off that he didn't tell me that before, but in a way it is probably better. He is right about one thing. I would have been worried as hell thinking about it on top of worrying about the surgery and recovery. No sense in thinking about it now. It's something down the road.

"They put that port in up here, and they can do everything through there. Blood tests, IV, meds, everything so you don't have to get stuck anymore." She is pointing toward my left shoulder where all of the tubes are coming from. I feel a little pressure there and some tape pulling on my chest hairs, but no pain. Port. That is what they use to give you chemo. He knew that was going to be necessary from the beginning and used my needle phobia as a bullshit reason when he told me he was going to put it in there. Now is not the time to get aggravated. And I'm not. I feel foggy and groggy but unusually content. I have no pain, and the reality that the surgery is over makes me feel a tinge of relief. Yes, I know recovery is the tough part, but so far it's a breeze. That won't last, but I'll take it for now.

I usually get very antsy when I am not in control. Laying there in a drug induced state of contentment, I realize that all of these people around me are taking total care of me. I can't get up, can't walk, can barely talk. I have nowhere to go, and no one requires anything of me at this moment. Time is meaningless. I don't know what time it is, and I don't care. I resolve to just let time do what time does... Pass.

Time is what I am going to need to get better and start living a normal life again. Do I dare start thinking about the rest of my life? Am I now safe to plan on *having* a rest of my life? Do I define the rest of my life in terms of years or is that too ambitious?

My heart tells me that I am beating this. Everything, for the most part, has been positive up to this point so why should I believe that it won't continue? Maybe it's the drugs but right now, as I lay here in a recovery room, knowing that the ugly, fear invoking bloody tumor in the picture that landed in my lap on October 4th is out of me...I think everything is going to be ok.

I'm not sure when I fell asleep, but I am waking up in a much quieter place. My eyes start to focus, and the bright lights and commotion I experienced in the recovery room are gone. The room is actually pretty dark with just a light hue coming from the door to my right.

I hear beeping and a few muffled voices outside but not much else. It must be the night. I must be alone now. Then I hear Nancy's voice speaking to me very softly as she touches my arm. "Hi honey, how you feeling?" I think I am smiling because I am so comforted to know she is here with me. "So far so good," I say. "What time is it?" I ask as if it matters. "About 7:00. You've been sleeping since they brought you in here. I think they have you pretty loaded up with pain meds". Well, they must be working because I don't feel any pain at all. Hell, I don't really feel much of anything except the warm touch of my wife's hand on my arm.

"Dr. Matthews is supposed to be here in a few minutes and then he is leaving for Japan." She says. Wait. Did she just say he is leaving for JAPAN? Where does that leave me? What if something goes wrong. I feel my heart start to beat a little faster, and I am sure the look on my face reflected my concern. "He said his partners would be here to visit you every day until you go home, and he would see you when he gets back. He said all you have to do now is rest and let your body recover". I'm sure she was trying to alleviate my concerns, but I still didn't like the sound of it.

I went through a long process of deciding on this guy as my doctor and now that I put all of my faith and trust in him to take care of me he bolts off to Japan. I have to hope that his partners are as good as he is. I guess there is nothing I can do about it.

Even though I am in a bit of a fog from the medications and the ordeal I have just been through, the unmistakable sound of Dr. Matthews's voice outside my door gets my heart racing again. The raspy, almost slurring cadence of his voice has become all too familiar to me and knowing that he is coming in to see me makes me feel a little anxious. Damn, but I wish he weren't going to freaking Japan. Maybe I'll tell him that. Yeah, like it would matter.

“Hey, it's over. That ought to make you feel better”. He is still in his teal scrubs, and as my eyes catch his, I can’t help but think he looks really tired. I don’t even know how long ago it was that he operated on me, and I know that he had several other surgeries today besides mine. For just a moment I think about how difficult his job is. Cutting into people’s bodies. Dealing with life and death day in and day out. Dealing with the families. I already have enormous respect for the guy, but in that brief moment, I am hit with profound gratitude. It wells up inside me, and I feel like I might start to cry.

“Hell, I wasn’t sure you were ever gonna pull the trigger, but now that we got that thing out of there, I feel really good that it went so well. We’ll just have to wait for the pathology report, but I am pretty optimistic. Got great margins and all in all it went about how I expected. How ya feeling?”

His rambling jolts me back to the moment, and I smile and say “pretty stoned. What’s this crap about you leaving me and going to Japan?”

“Yeah, I’m going to be gone for a couple of weeks, but “Nas” and the other doctors will be here taking good care of you. You’ll be out of here in a couple of days and then all you have to do is relax and get your strength back. We’ve already got you set up with an appointment to come into the office on the 10th and get the staples out so I'll see you then. Quit worrying Colachicco, geez."

The volume of his voice drops as he turns to talk to Nan. I am not sure what they are saying, but I see Nan force a smile. Hopefully, it is something worth smiling about and not another one of Dr. Matthews's dumb ass jokes.

I want to close my eyes now. I come to the quick conclusion that everything I just heard is the full extent of the amount of information I will receive. That conclusion moves my focus back to the overwhelming feeling of fatigue that is permeating my body, and frankly my mind.

"Ok boss, you're good to go. Just rest and do what everybody tells you. Your port is in so you won't need to get stuck every five minutes while you're in here. Quit worrying, and I'll see you in a couple of weeks."

And with that, Dr. Matthews is gone.

"How ya feeling honey?" Nan sits down in the big chair situated next to my bed. She puts her hand on my elbow, and for some reason, I am surprised that I can feel it. Weird. For some reason I guess I thought that between the anesthesia and the pain meds I wouldn't be able to feel anything.

"Pretty whipped," I say with a sigh.

"He's a hoot isn't he?" she says.

“Yeah, what were you guys talking about?”

“He was just telling me that it would take 3 or 4 days to get the pathology report back and that someone from his office would call me when it came in. He said he was optimistic, but nothing is definite until they see the pathology report.”

What the hell takes so long with these tests? Is there actually something about the test that takes time to happen or am I just in line with dozens of other people waiting to have their tumors analyzed? I guess it’s the latter. Nothing I can do about that, so I just settle in and try to forget about it.

“You might as well go. I’m probably going to just go to sleep” I say to Nan.

Before she has a chance to answer, the door opens, and I see light streaming into the room. A young man, looks to be about 30 comes in, and he is wearing scrubs. I don’t recognize him as one of Dr. Matthews’s people so I just say “Hello.”

With a big smile, he says “Hey Mr. Dan, I’m Matt, and I’m going to be your night nurse”.

Great. My first night in the hospital and my nurse is a guy. Not sure why that gives me pause, and I know it shouldn’t but the word “Nurse” and “Guy” don’t seem to go together in my mind. He smiles wider and shakes Nancy’s hand. There is a rolling stool that I had not seen until this point when Matt rolls it up next to my bed. Although I am lying at about a 30-degree angle, Matt and I are just about eye to eye.

“You’re probably shaking off the effects of the anesthesia by now. You look good. Let’s take your vitals”.

He starts doing his thing with the blood pressure thingy and sticking that temperature probe in my ear. He puts another plastic thing on my finger, and various beeps begin to sound. I don’t know what they mean and really couldn’t care less. I start checking out Matt who is going to be caring for me all night I guess.

He’s got the obligatory stethoscope hanging around his neck and a couple of badges and tags attached to his scrubs. There is a phone or walkie talkie sticking out of his pocket. He is wearing a lanyard with his ID attached to it. The lanyard is adorned with the University of Alabama logo along with an Alabama pin of some sort.

“Bama fan I see,” I said as he unwrapped the Velcro strap from the blood pressure machine.

“Big time. Big game this weekend against Georgia. Hope you’re not a Georgia fan, I might have to hurt you” he says with a big smile.

“Nope. Really don’t care about that game, but I’ll root for Bama if you take good care of me” I say right back at him.

“Deal,” he says.

Matt seems like one of those guys who has a perpetual smile on his face.

“Let’s check out the surgical area. I’m going to move your gown to the side here and take a look”.

As Matt carefully moves the hospital gown, I look down to see that the area from just below my chest to my pubic line is wrapped with what looks like packing tape. I can’t say that I really feel it on there, but it looks weird. All the hair has been shaved off, and there are 4 or 5 gauze patches under the tape. All I can think about is how much it is going to hurt when they take that sucker off.

Matt is moving his stethoscope around and isn’t smiling quite as much. I’m sure it is because he is concentrating on what he hears through the stethoscope and not because he is concerned. I hope.

“On a scale of one to ten, with 10 being the worst, what is your level of pain, Dan?”

I give it some thought and try to do a quick assessment. I have no pain. None. Zero. Zilch. But I should, right? I can’t say zero, I will sound ridiculous since I just had major cancer surgery a few hours ago.

“Probably 3 or 4,” I say sheepishly.

"Ok. You're on some pretty strong pain meds, so I think we'll be able to keep it under control for you. You need anything?"

I am starting to like this guy. He's a "regular guy" and I feel very comfortable with him.

"So far, so good," I say. "What time is it?"

"About 8 o'clock. Why? You got a plane to catch or something?"

I actually chuckle a little. "You and I are going to get along just fine, Matt."

His big smile is back. "You bet, Dan. Just go ahead and get some rest. I'm putting this call box right here next to your arm and wrapping it around the bed rail. If you need anything, just push this button, and the nurse's station will answer. Tell them what you need, and we'll take care of it. I'll be back in a few."

The call box seems to be within easy reach, and I put my hand on it just to be sure that I can. No problem. The door to my room slowly closes as Matt heads off to take care of another patient. I look around the dimly lit room. I'm all alone. I am not afraid, just tired. I close my eyes and let sleep take over my body.

The big heavy door to my room swings open. I hear the squeak of Matt's sneakers walking toward my bed. It's still dark. I can't tell how long I've been sleeping, but I wish I still was. The adrenaline starts to pump as I wonder what this visit is about.

"Time to check your vitals buddy," Matt says.

"Didn't we just do that?"

"Every three hours. I let you sleep so it's been 5 hours. You don't wanna get me fired now do you?"

Matt is once again wrapping the blood pressure band around my arm and doing his thing. Five hours. Damn. It didn't feel like five hours. So it's the middle of the night. He's going to wake me up every three hours? That sucks. Seems like one of the many ironies about being hospitalized. All I had heard before I went to sleep was "get rest, get rest, get rest" and then they wake you up every three hours to make sure that while you were "resting" your blood pressure and temperature didn't go up. I shouldn't complain, they know what they're doing....I hope.

This time, Matt has a tray with a variety of things on it, one of which is a rather larger syringe.

"I have to get some blood, but we draw it through the port." He gently touches my left shoulder in the general direction of the taped up tubes protruding from my chest. He pokes the needle into a plastic piece about 12 inches down the tube, and I see the crimson hemoglobin filling the clear tube attached to the needle.

As I watch, I take a moment and thank God that this little piece of plastic implanted under my skin is going to spare me the many, many pokes that I dread as I go through this recovery. Then it hits me that the real reason for the port is to administer chemo, and I feel the anxiety rush over me again. It quickly passes as I hear Matt's voice.

"Did you get some sleep?"

"I was in la la land until you came in here and woke my ass up. How does everything look so far?"

"Exactly as it should," he says with another big smile. He puts labels on three tubes of my blood, writes on them and puts them on the little metal tray by my bed. He puts them into a clear plastic package with yet another label attached.

"Be right back?" he says as he walks out into the brightly lit hallway. After about five minutes he is back, empty handed this time. He rolls the little stool up next to my bed and sits down next to me.

"How's the pain?"

"3, maybe 3 and a half," I say, failing at my attempt to come up with a humorous answer. Matt gives a half-hearted chuckle anyway.

"Let's get you up for a minute."

He has to be kidding. He's still smiling, but I can clearly tell that he is NOT kidding. Does he not know that I just had surgery? Of course, he does.

"Is this something that is absolutely necessary Matt? I mean I feel all cozy and cushy here, and it is what, 2 o'clock in the morning? Why don't you check with me in the morning or perhaps in a week or two?"

Matt doesn't acknowledge my sarcasm but instead starts to pull back the covers off of my bed. As I look down at my body, I am a bit surprised to see just how many tubes are sticking out of me.

"The Doc's always want to see you get up the same day as surgery. It's good for you and accelerates the healing process. I'll hold on to you, and it's not like you have to run around the block. Just get up and take a couple of steps for me. A piece of cake and then you can go back to sleep for a while. It's just about time for your pain meds so that will help you relax too. C'mon. Let's do it, Dan."

I am very unsure of this, but I can see that Matt is not going to back down. He puts his hands on my ankles and tells me to pivot around slowly, and he'll prop me up.

"Just get into a sitting position that you are as comfortable as possible in and I'll help you to your feet from there." He says.

I feel the movement of my lower body, and I don't have any pain to speak of. As promised he braces my back as my feet hang over the edge of the hospital bed and touch the floor. I am starting to believe I can do this, not that I really have a choice. With a little pressure on my back from Matt's hands, I manage to get vertical. Not bad. I actually feel fairly normal other than the pulling of the packing tape across my belly and a little pain in my abdomen area.

"I don't dance Matt so don't even ask."

"Take a couple of steps toward me. Don't worry, I gotcha!"

Matt has one hand on my forearm, and the other is around my back. I take a step and hear the sound of the wheeled stand holding bags of fluids rolling with me. Matt is pushing it with the hand he has around my back.

As I take the extremely small step, I feel a bit light headed, but I don't say anything. Maybe it will pass. I stop after two steps and just let myself stand still for a minute. The pulling around my abdomen area is quickly turning into pain, and I feel like my insides are being pummeled with needles.

"Ok, I need to get back into bed Matt. Is this enough to satisfy the docs?"

"Yeah. Just turn a bit toward me, and I'll help you get back into bed. Good job Dan."

With that, I feel Matt guiding me back toward the bed, and I feel myself almost drop back onto the thin mattress. I wedge my left foot up on the frame of the hospital bed, and Matt does the rest, lifting my legs up and straightening me out on the bed. I'm totally exhausted, and I am not going to wait for Matt to ask me about my pain level.

"My pain went from 3 to 9 there Matt. Keep this up, and I am going to become a Georgia fan just to piss you off." I say with labored breath.

"Ok, we can't have that. Let me get you something for the pain."

I close my eyes for what seemed like only a few seconds, but when I opened them again, I see Matt putting another needle into the plastic piece on my port tube. It takes less than five seconds before I feel a warm and fuzzy feeling wash over my body like a blanket. My thoughts become less clear, but I feel an unusual feeling of contentment. I like it. The thoughts and feelings of pain quickly become non-existent, and I know it is time to sleep. Matt knows this too, and I hear him say something about coming back before his shift ends. I am fading in and out, but at one point I scan the room and accept the realization that I am once again alone. I choose to make this my signal to sleep and slowly close my eyes.

November 28, 2012

What the hell is all of that noise? I hear a static-laden voice over a speaker of some sort, women laughing and a general clambering of items banging together. I am annoyed and confused. The room looks different now. It is light outside, and the gray hue penetrating through the white shade over my window makes my room look much clearer than when I scoped it out the night before. Maybe it's the drugs.

I notice a clock on the wall directly in front of my bed. 7:00 straight up. A new day. My first day without that freaking tumor inside of me. It is like crossing a bridge, and now I am on the other side. Yes, there is still uncertainty, but I can't help acknowledge my relief. I made it through the surgery. Everybody has positive things to say. I actually stood up last night. I am starting to recover. Hell yeah! This is what optimism feels like.

I position my hands below my hips and try to scoot myself up in the bed. I manage about an inch or two, and the extreme effort to do so doesn't seem worth it. My ass is sore, and I feel like this stupid hospital gown is twisted around me like a burrito wrap. Whatever these women are laughing at outside my room, it must be pretty good because it has gotten louder. As quickly as the thought enters my mind, their voices fade off, and I can only hear the continued sound of glass and metal clanging together.

The door swings open, and a woman is backing into my room. As she clears the door jam, I see she is carrying a tray with plastic covers over the plates.

"Breakfast for you," she says without looking at me. She seems to hesitate about where to put the tray and quickly settles on sliding it onto the rolling table next to my bed. A variety of items from sippy cups to papers slide to the end of the table as she pushes the tray across the top. I glance outside the door and see other women in scrubs grabbing trays off a cart and scurrying in different directions. I now know what all that racket was outside my door.

My breakfast delivery person spins around and leaves as abruptly as she entered pulling the door shut behind her. I hear the sound of the cart fade off as they roll it down the hall away from my room. I can't decide if I prefer the quite or liked the sound of activity in my general vicinity. There is some slight comfort in knowing that day to day people are going about their jobs around me. It is a feeling of normalness that I kind of like.

I can smell the food even though it is still covered. There are two plastic containers which are sealed, but I can read what is printed on them. One is orange juice and the other is apple sauce. I also see a small bowl of Jell-O covered with plastic wrap. I think about taking the plastic lid off the plate but I can't. I am suddenly hit with a twinge of anxiety about this moment, and the questions start peppering my brain.

"I am hooked up to all of these tubes and wires……can I even move my arms enough to reach across and feed myself"?

"Am I allowed to eat this stuff"? "What if I choke"?

I'm not even hungry, so I just let it all sit there. Damn, I almost feel paralyzed even though I know I'm not. I wonder when Matt will be in here? I'm not really feeling any pain, but I can't help hoping for more pain medication. I'd rather be drugged up before the pain comes than wait until I am hurting.

I look at the clock. 7:20. Time moves so slowly when you are laying in a hospital bed. I think about the last 24 hours. At this time yesterday I was still at home preparing for the big day. Since then, I've had the tumor removed, stood up, met Matt, got introduced to some serious pain medication and been served breakfast in bed. All things considered, I fared pretty well to this point.

That makes me chuckle, and I start thinking maybe that breakfast is a good idea after all. I test out my right arm by moving it out from under the thin blanket and raising it up to my face. That was easy. I assess the length of the tubes protruding from my bandaged hand and decide I can reach the tray without a problem. Still, I do so very slowly just in case I miscalculated.

Without even thinking about it I remove the lid from the plate. Scrambled eggs and buttered toast. Ok, now I am hungry. With my confidence gaining, I maneuver the tray across the top of my lap so that everything is right in front of me. I can do this.

There is silverware in a paper sleeve, and I slide it out onto the tray. I pick up the fork and dig into the eggs. Luke warm but not bad. I pick up the toast and take a bite. I ate for what seemed like a half an hour, even managing to use both hands to open the sealed orange juice container.

Eating felt good but wore me out. When I decided to put the fork down and declare myself finished, I looked at the tray. Half the eggs were still there, and one slice of toast was left. I didn't eat much but felt like I had enjoyed a feast. "the first accomplishment of the day" I declared to no one there.

I pushed the tray away from the bed and laid back on the pillow. I could still taste the food in my mouth although it was not a natural taste. There was almost a medicinal flavor to it. Whatever. I don't recall falling asleep, but I do remember waking up to the door slamming against the backstop. A big guy with a lab coat on comes lumbering in and positions himself at the foot of my bed.

"Hey man, how ya doing?" he says as he grabs a clipboard that apparently was hanging off the end of my bed. "I'm Dr. Nelson, I was with Dr. Matthews during your surgery, remember?"

Is he kidding? Do I remember him? I wanted to crack a joke but couldn't come up with anything, so I just said: "Oh yeah."

Dr. Nelson seems to just glance at the chart and then walks up next to my bed. He rolls a small stool toward me that I hadn't noticed until now, and slides it under his butt in a single motion. Without a word he pulls the blanket down and pulls my hospital gown up just under my neck.

"Let's have a look," he says as his eyes focus in on my midsection.

I look down and for the first time I see Dr. Matthews's handy work. The packing tape covers most of my midsection from below my belly button, across my rib cage and up to my pectoral muscles. Under the tape, I see the three gauze bandages, including one directly over my belly button. Before I have a chance to process what I just saw, Dr. Nelson pulls my gown back down and pulls the covers about half way back up.

"I see you ate. Have you had a bowel movement yet?" Is he serious? I had surgery on my colon and rectum less than 24 hours ago, and you want to know if I have had a bowel movement? I can't imagine what that first one is going to be like. Is it going to hurt? All of a sudden I am sorry I ate solid food.

"Uh, no, doc. Not something I have really thought about. I'm just getting used to the idea of standing." He doesn't laugh, and I barely finish the sentence before he says "Are you passing gas? You're probably farting a lot."

I have to think now.

"I'm not really sure, Doc."

"You don't know if you passed gas?"

"I've had my mind on a few other things." I try not to sound overly sarcastic because I am not sure if he is kidding or not.

"Yeah, man, I get that, but it's important to know that all the plumbing is working down there. Try to take note of how much you are passing gas and let the nurse know when you take a crap."

He has a half-hearted smile, like using the word "crap" makes him more relatable. I guess it actually does in a weird way.

"Hey doc, do I need to be careful about what I eat? I had some eggs and toast a few minutes ago, and I feel like I had a feast."

"Your appetite will improve as you get better. Drink a lot of water and eat as much as you can when they bring it. You can order stuff you like off the menu. You're doing just fine. Either I or one of our partners will be back tomorrow to check on you. Hang in there buddy!"

And with that Dr. Nelson stands, the backs of his knees pushing the wheeled stool away in no particular direction and he bolts out the door. Interesting guy. I immediately decide that I don't like him as well as Dr. Matthews, and I wish Dr. Matthews weren't halfway around the world as I lay here recovering.

My thoughts turn to Dr. Nelson's questions about bowel movements and passing gas. I should have asked him why it is important to know if I fart or not. What if I wasn't farting and didn't have a bowel movement for a couple of days? What does that mean? I'll ask him tomorrow and who knows, maybe I'll fart my brains out and take a nice poop between now and then.

November 29, 2012

"Hi, I'm Sam," says the pretty young nurse who has entered my room. I've been fading in and out of consciousness throughout the night and now realize that the sun is up. Sam is the new nurse who came on at 7 a.m., relieving the tall skinny one who didn't talk much but woke me up every three hours to take my vital signs. As I gain a bit of clarity, I look up at the clock on the wall. It's 8:20. Maybe I slept more than I thought.

"I'm going to be giving you a Lovenox injection this morning. Have you had a bowel movement?"

The second question is easy to answer but what was that first thing she said? Injection?

"No bowel movement yet. What's Lovenox?" I ask.

"It is to prevent blood clots after surgery. I can inject it into your thigh or your stomach. Most people prefer the thigh."

Sam obviously doesn't know that I have a port. That magic passage implanted into my chest that allows me to avoid becoming a pin cushion.

"I have a port so you can go through there, right?"

"No, the Lovenox is a direct injection. It can't be administered through the port."

Hold the phone, sister! Are you sure about that? What the hell difference would it make if the shit goes in through a puncture wound in my skin or this very useful plastic device connected to my blood stream?

"The doctor didn't say anything to me about getting an injection. Are you sure it is necessary? I mean do I have a choice in the matter?" I'm sure I sound pathetic. I know my voice is weak, and the fear of that needle in my stomach or my thigh must make me sound very nervous.

"It is pretty standard after a surgery like yours. Blood clots are a big risk, and you definitely don't want that. It isn't as bad as it sounds. Most people tolerate it just fine."

Time to come clean. It is no longer embarrassing for me to say it out loud.

"I have a serious needle phobia. That's why Dr. Matthews wanted me to have the port. Can we wait on the injection until I have a chance to talk to the doctor about it?"

"We really shouldn't wait. You were supposed to have the first one yesterday," Sam says firmly.

"What do you mean first one?" I ask.

"You'll get one every morning that you are here. At least 3 injections. They are really important," Sam says.

"I believe you Sam, but I really want to talk to the doctor first. He should be here any minute." Of course, I had no idea when he would be there, but if he came in the morning like yesterday, it sounded like a logical assumption. "I can give you your pain meds through the port before the injection. That should make it much easier and also relieve any anxiety you have."

She obviously didn't hear a word I said about talking to the doctor first. She was beginning to look less pretty to me by the minute.

Sam, trying to encourage me, says, "You are due for your Dilaudid at 9. We'll give it a few minutes to take effect and then I'll come back. Sound good?"

HELL NO IT DOESN'T SOUND GOOD. What is Dilaudid anyway? I think I remember Nan saying that was the name of the pain medication. If that's the stuff they have been giving me I love it. Is that bad? I love my pain medication? I wonder if it is addictive. Maybe if she gives me a good dose of that stuff, I won't feel the injection.

Anyway, at least I have a reprieve until 9:30 or so. Maybe the doc will visit by then, and I can talk him out of it. Although I sure as hell don't want a blood clot. The anxiety is building, and I feel my face getting flush. My stomach is rumbling, and I don't know if it is hunger or nerves.

"Breakfast should be here shortly, and I'll be back at 9 to give you your Dilaudid. Any nausea?" Right now I am feeling a little wonky, so I say "yeah, a little."

"Ok, then I will get you something for that too," Sam replies.

They have a freaking drug for everything. I have come to the conclusion that the solution to almost every problem in the medical world is either to cut you open or give you drugs.

Sam leaves the room, and I am once again alone with my thoughts. It's been less than 48 hours since my surgery, but it feels like months. I am more alert right now than I have been since surgery so I decide to take stock of my condition.

Pain level? I focus on my incision area and other than the chafing of the tape and bandages, I really can't say I have any pain there. This kind of amazes me. I try to think about my internal organs. I think about the area that I imagine they cut into and removed during surgery. No pain there either. The only discomfort I really feel is my butt and lower back.

I feel the urge to scoot up in the bed, but I pause to consider whether or not this is a good idea. I still have all of these wires and tubes coming out of everywhere and I sure as hell don't want to dislodge anything. With a burst of confidence, I brace my hands below my hips and push my body upwards toward the top of the bed.

My butt slides out of the position it seemed to be stuck in, and I get immediate relief. My back seems to be better supported, and my lower body is much more comfortable. Cool. I did it. Thank goodness for small accomplishments.

It is 9:20 and I am pissed off that Sam has not returned at the promised time. Am I in need of the pain medication? Not really but she said she would be here at 9:00. She said she would give me the pain medication before stabbing me with that needle. Maybe I should hit my nurse's call button and start raising hell. No, I am not doing that. I close my eyes and wrestle my mind back under control. This is a classic example of the things that I used to stress over which are really not important. Even now that the surgery is over, I will need to keep reminding myself not to sweat the small stuff as they say.

I force myself to let go of the frustration and anxiety. I conjure up a smile and tell myself that Sam will be here when she gets here, and there is nothing to get riled up over. I relax my face, neck, and shoulders. Much better. Be in the moment. I am being cared for in this hospital, and that cancerous tumor is out of my body. I am recovering and getting better as time passes.

This one-sided conversation feels good, and I am proud of myself for grasping control over my emotions. With my eyes closed, I could almost doze off again. Why not? The rest is good for me. But if I sleep all day I might be up all night. Again, stop worrying. Just go with it.

With my mind and body feeling very much at rest I can start to sense my mind drifting toward sleep. Pain check? Zip. The bed actually feels comfortable right now.

I didn't hear Sam enter the room, but I could smell her clean skin, indicating she was very close to me. As my eyes slowly open, I see her pushing the last bit of syringe into the plastic device attached to the tube which will deliver it into my veins. Before I could speak, that incredible, warm wave engulfed my body from head to toe. I just wanted to say "Ahhhh Yeah, this feels awesome" but I decided it wasn't worth the effort.

"I also gave you Zofran for nausea," Sam says, assuming I knew she had just given me the pain meds. I forgot about nausea, and as the pain meds sent my mind into a state of Utopia, I couldn't really figure out if the nausea was real or imagined. I also didn't care.

"I'll be back in about an hour, and we'll get you up." Sam pivots and leaves without even a friendly farewell gesture. An hour. Sounds good. I'll just enjoy the high I am feeling right now and let that hour pass at its own pace. I have no recollection of falling asleep.

"Dan? Why don't you have some water and we'll get you into that chair for a while?" Sam and a muscular gent are standing to my immediate right. They want me to stand? Yeah, I don't think so. I just got comfortable, and I am still quite stoned from the medication.

"We have to do this now?" I ask

"Walking is critical to your recovery, Dan. Doctor's orders. You can do this. Marcus is going to help you up, and we are going to walk over to the chair. Don't worry about your IV, I've got it. Do you feel like you need to use the bathroom first?"

"No. I'm still pretty groggy," I reply.

"Ok, well we've got you." Sam and Marcus go to work lowering the side of the hospital bed and maneuvering the rolling IV stand. Sam has my ankles, and Marcus is hovering over me with his hand on my shoulder.

"I'll help you lower your feet to the floor. Can you push yourself up enough to stand?" asks Marcus.

I'm not talking now just trying to follow instructions. As I manage to get vertical, I am somewhat amazed at how strong I feel. Maybe it's the drugs making me feel invincible. Marcus has me under the arm, and the upward pressure combined with my noble efforts result in me standing pretty effortlessly. I take a second to recognize my accomplishment and then Sam gently takes my other arm.

"Let's walk over to the chair. Nice and easy, one step at a time. We've got you." I love being spoken to like I am 3 years old.

I shuffle my feet across the floor and tell myself I am walking. After some strides, I am around the bed and standing in front of the chair. Marcus tugs me to one side indicating that he wants me to prepare to sit. Another challenge. He wraps his forearm around my back and supports my gentle fall into the big chair. Made it.

I rest my arms on the cushioned arms of the chair and lay my head back enjoying the sensation of sitting up straight for the first time post-surgery. I think my eyes were closed, but I am suddenly hit with a sharp sting in the top of my right leg. Oh no, I must have pulled something walking over.

My eyes dart down to the site of the pain, and I see Sam removing the syringe from my upper thigh. *You sneaky little bitch. You never said a word.* She pops up and heads toward the door.

"I'll be back in a bit to check on you. Don't try to get up by yourself. I put the nurse's call button next to you on the chair." And with that she was gone. I wanted to give her a few choice words for her deception, but she didn't give me a chance. I look down at the freshly punctured spot on my leg and come to the realization that it really didn't hurt that bad. Maybe it was because I didn't know it was coming. I've often wondered if my whole needle phobia was more about the anticipation than the actual pain associated with getting stuck.

I am out of bed. I am in a chair, vertical and for a fleeting moment, I enjoy the notion of being normal again. The warmth of the sun coming through the window hits my face, and I take notice. In fact, I start to take notice of everything around me…where I've come from to get to this point and where I go from here. The solitude of the moment hits me. I don't experience many of these quiet times alone, but they bring feelings of peace and serenity. I know I am getting better, but I don't know what the next steps are now that surgery is over. The CT scan said cancer hadn't spread to any of my other organs. God, that seems like an eternity ago since I got that news. But why does Dr. Matthews think I will need chemotherapy? The thought of it sends shivers down my spine. I made it this far and did pretty well if I do say so myself. I can handle whatever comes next. I may not have a choice.

I'm kind of proud of myself for how I have handled this ordeal to this point. Cancer is such a horrible word. It almost implies death. I think everyone knows someone who has died of cancer. My Mom died of lung cancer. Dad had prostate cancer, Uncle Jim had pancreatic cancer, my friend Jay….. I could create a pretty long list, and I'm sure that is typical for most people.

People who beat cancer are called "survivors." To use that term as a label for people who did not die from cancer naturally implies that people who get cancer are *supposed to die*. So if you don't….you survived. I hope to be able to call myself a survivor. I like the word. It has power and reflects accomplishment. I decide that I am going to label myself a survivor as of this very moment. It feels good.

I scoot up to get comfortable in the chair, and my back touches the cold leather (or more likely, vinyl) of the chair. These hospital gowns are designed by sadomasochistic trolls who design enough open area in strategic places on the garment to cause maximum embarrassment. I wonder where my clothes are? Not that I can put them on but I wonder where all the stuff I had when I got here went. Maybe Nan has it. Maybe I can get her to bring me a robe.

The thought of her being here makes me both happy and sad at the same time. I want her to see me sitting up in this chair. She will see that I am getting stronger. I wish she were here right now. She has been so strong and so supportive through this whole ordeal. I'm sure my fear and frustration caused me to be an asshole from time to time, and I know she took the brunt of that.

As if she didn't have her hands full enough taking care of her mom every day, now she has me and my cancer to deal with. I don't even want to think about the times she spent worrying about what her life would be like if I died. How she would survive financially because I failed to get us life insurance. I am so pissed at myself for putting her through that. I close my eyes and ask God to give me a chance to make it up to her.

I want the strength to fight and maybe a dash of luck so that I can right my wrongs. I want to get through this and give my family the life they deserve, and I want to be around to see them enjoy as much of it as I can. A feeling of resolve bubbles up inside me, and I am almost brought to tears with determination. *I'm a survivor. I'm a survivor.* I can do this and I freaking will.

I feel like I have been sitting in this chair for hours, but it has only been 45 minutes. There are tubes and wires protruding from under my hospital gown and going in several directions. They are connected to things that are hanging on this metal tree contraption, and they range from beeping electronic devices to a bevy of labeled bags containing various levels of fluids.

As I survey all of this stuff, I try to feel where on my body each thing is attached to. I am a hairy guy, and the nodes that are adhered to my chest and belly remind me of that fact. I can see one of them on my chest, and it has what appears to be a little battery cable attached to it. Annoying, but not really painful.

There is a tube coming from my crotch area with yellowish liquid coming from it. I know what that is and try to generate some feeling "down there." Nothing. Just as well I think. There is a mass of bandages between my left collar bone and my arm pit which is where the now infamous "port" is located. The clear tube with the insertion device extends from the bandages and seeing it somehow gives me a sigh of relief. This is Dr. Matthews's solution for saving me from a virtually endless series of needle punctures. Injections go in.....blood draws come out. No fuss, no muss. Thanks, doc, good plan.

I look up at the bags of fluids and see that one is completely empty. Hope that isn't something that is keeping me alive. Maybe I should tell Sam. Then again, I'm not quite ready to welcome her back into my life after the little stabbing incident. If I am honest, it wasn't that bad. Maybe the pain meds did their job, or maybe I was just overacting. Perhaps I'll cut Sam some slack.

Something tells me that I am ready to get back into bed. I'm over the thrill of conquering the chair and fatigue is setting in. Should I try to do this myself or call a nurse? Before I have a chance to make that decision, a doctor walks in carrying a metal clipboard with a stack of papers attached to it. I haven't seen him before, at least I don't remember seeing him before. His skin tone indicates that he is middle eastern or perhaps Indian.

"Hello Don, I am Dr. Morrey. I work with Doctors Matthews and Nelson."

Yup, definitely middle eastern. I'm not going to correct him on my name, but I hope if he is reading it from his stack of papers that it is the only mistake written there.

"It is good to see you up. How are you feeling today?" he says.

"Pretty good. It was good to get out of that bed and into a vertical position. I'm a little tired right now though so if you can help me get back into the bed that'd be swell."

He looks surprised at my request.

"Sure, sure, I can get someone to help you back into bed."

Really? Like this is beneath you? "*Oh, I'm a Doctor…. Helping you get up and back into bed ain't in my job description. I have peeps for that*". Jeez.

"Have you had a bowel movement today?" the doctor asks.

I pull up my gown from the side and look down at my butt.

"Let me check," I say. This guy has no sense of humor as he stares at me with a blank stone face. "No doc, I haven't had a bowel movement today."

Dr. Morrey is writing on his clipboard, and his face is expressionless. I wonder how many patients he has to see this morning for Dr. Matthews? I wonder how he keeps up with all of their treatments, how they're recovering, what they need, etc. I've never seen this guy. My history is with Dr. Matthews. Can he really know everything he needs to know about what I've gone through, and continue to go through, from that stupid metal clipboard stacked with papers? *Doctoring really is a business* I think to myself. That makes me a little angry and nervous at the same time. Hopefully, he knows what he's doing.

"How's your pain? On a scale of 1 – 10 with 10 being the worst?"

"Well, it was pretty good until my new friend Sam came in here and impaled my thigh with a syringe filled with Lovenox. Right now I'd say my pain is about a 4, but it's hard to say because I am feeling pretty uncomfortable in this chair right now. When do you think you can have someone help me back into bed, doc?"

I figured I'd nudge the point a bit.

"Yes, um, the Lovenox. It is to prevent you from getting blood clots after surgery. It is very important. I can help you get back into bed. If you can stand. I will move everything with you. You can hold on to me to steady yourself. Are you ready?"

I'm not feeling overly confident in this offer from the good doctor, but I really want to get back into bed. I survey the wires and tubes to make sure I'm not obstructing anything or risking an accidental pull. Pushing myself up out of the chair was pretty easy, but the minute I was on my feet I started feeling lightheaded. I grabbed the doc's shoulder and eyed my target... The bed.

I shuffled toward the bed and almost immediately found myself out of breath. My abdomen felt like I had swallowed a beach ball. The Doctor rolled the tree with all of the equipment and fluids on it toward the bed at the same pace that I was moving. I slowly pivoted and maneuvered my butt up against the plastic mattress. Feeling contact, I plopped myself down. The tape across my abdomen and the sticking nodes on my torso pulled and stung. Dr. Morrey was lifting my legs up and swinging them around so that I would end up once again horizontal. It didn't feel good, but there was a significant level of comfort as I settled into my bed.

"I'd say the pain level just went up to about a 7 doc."

No response from Dr. Morrey. Funny, he seemed interested a few minutes ago. I do appreciate the fact that he helped me back into the bed though, and I am now reminded of the trauma I have been through. The strength and exhilaration I felt an hour ago when I made it into the chair is a distant memory, and right now I just want to lay here and let people take care of me. Either that or I want to go to sleep.

"You are on a regular regimen to control the pain, and you have the pump here. We will make sure that stays under control. Have you eaten today? How's your appetite?"

Did I eat today? My head is fuzzy, and I'm not really sure. That's kind of scary.

"I've been eating. Can't say that I am really hungry but when I eat it tastes good. Not a lot of food but a little bit every time they bring it."

That seemed like a reasonable answer.

"Ok. Well, I want you to get up and move around to the best of your ability several times a day. Eat well to get your strength up. Dr. Nelson will be in later, and he will talk to you about the discharge procedure."

Discharge procedure? They are thinking about sending me home?

"Discharge as in going home?" I ask.

“You will recover better at home. Statistics prove it out. Dr. Nelson will discuss it with you.”

I don’t want to think about this right now. Hearing what the doctor just told me makes my heart start racing, and I feel flush. Frankly, it scares me. As much as I love the idea of being out of the hospital, something tells me that it is just too soon to think about going home. When was my surgery? Yesterday? The day before? Just trying to process all of this is exhausting.

“Ok. Take care. It looks like you’re doing great.” And with that, Dr. Morrey is out the door.

I’m alone again, and I close my eyes. I wonder what time it is? I begrudgingly open my right eye and focus in on the clock. 11:40. It has been a busy morning and now it’s time to take a nap. I quickly calculate the time since my last dose of pain medication. I’m ready for more. Not necessarily because I am in a lot of pain, but it feels so relaxing after they administer it, I think it will help me to sleep. I’ll call Sam and remind her. I hit the nurse's call button and wait for a response. The crackly voice answers quickly.

“Yes, what do you need?”

“I think it’s time for my pain meds.” I say.

“Ok, we will be in shortly.”

That was easy. I'll just close my eyes and wait for her to come in. With that, I fade off, and I still have no idea if Sam ever came in and gave me the pain medication. I was in a deep sleep.

November 29th, 2012
6:40 p.m.

The sound of my wife's voice is music to my ears. She has just come back from feeding her mom. It is her second visit to see me today. She was here from 12:30 until 2:30 during which time she got into a beef with Sam about not changing my empty IV and not giving me my meds on time. Then she drove the 20 miles or so north to take care of and feed her mom, and now she is back here with me.

My heart swells with an appreciation for her. What did I do to deserve this angel? Having her at my side right now just makes everything better. I pause for a moment to appreciate her effect on my senses. Her beautiful face and cheery attitude. The sound of her voice and the smell of her skin. The feeling of her hand on my shoulder. I will never take these things for granted again.

"I'll be glad to see the night shift nurse come on at 7:00. Did the guy this morning say what time the doctor will be here?"

"Nope. Just that he was going to talk to me about going home."

Almost on cue, Dr. Nelson comes lumbering into the room with a big smile and a towering voice. Everyone else around here seems to have some modicum of respect for not disturbing other patients, but Dr. Nelson knows how to make an entrance. He fixes his eyes right on me.

"Hey, big guy how ya doing? That port serving its purpose? I'll bet you love us for that right about now."

He turns to Nancy as he hears her forced laughter at his lame humor.

"Hi Ms. C. How's our boy doing?" he asks.

Treating it like a rhetorical question, Dr. Nelson pulls up the rolling stool next to my bed and starts manipulating the covers, tubes, and wires so that he can get into my hospital gown. After a few firm pokes at my abdomen much like a cat would knead a soft pillow, Dr. Nelson grabs hold of the plastic tape covering my belly and starts tearing it away. The sound is disconcerting and I can't help think *this has gotta hurt!!!*

"Awesome" is all he says as he pulls it away.

"Jeez doc, no warning? You just pulled that off me like you're unwrapping your latest delivery from Amazon!"

"What'd ya think we were going to do, leave it on there? Did you want to take it home with you? It did its job, and now it's gone. Boom! Ya gotta feel better with it off of there, right? So have you been eating? How are your bowel movements?"

Again with the freaking bowel movements. It's no longer did you have one, it's "How are your bowel movements?"

What the hell kind of question is that? *What kind of answer are you looking for dude?*

"I eat a little when they bring it. Lots of Jell-O. Not much in the crapping department. Is that bad?"

My belly still stings from him pulling that tape off, but I have to admit it is kind of liberating. Even though he covered me back up with my gown, I can feel the cool air tickling across my midsection.

"We need to know that you're moving your bowels before we can send you home. Doesn't have to be a fecal avalanche but you have to be pooping. That whole area of your life is going to get a little spastic from now on. But hey, look at the bright side. A lot of folks who go through what you went through come out of here with a bag on their hip. You dodged that bullet. Just do the best you can to get to the toilet and poop when you feel even the slightest urge."

'Fecal avalanche'? '...a little spastic?' What doctor talks like this?

"Ok doc, I'm not feeling much down in that area, but I'll give it a try. What's this about sending me home? What are you thinking?"

"You're going home tomorrow. How does that sound?" The doc says.

That uneasy feeling comes over me again, and I can tell my heart is racing a bit. Dr. Nelson is standing straight across from me, leaning against the food cart with his arms crossed. He's wearing full scrubs, and he's got the little surgery beanie on his head with the white straps hanging down on each side. I wonder if he just did surgery on someone and then popped in here to visit with me on his way out?

I try to process the thought of going home tomorrow so that I can decide if I like the idea or not. The concept is appealing because it represents recovery. Going home is the next logical step in defining recovery for me, and it indicates that I don't need to be in a hospital anymore.

At the same time, I've got all of this shit protruding from my body, and I have to assume that it is necessary for something, or they wouldn't have all these fluids going into my body and all of these wires monitoring whatever they are monitoring. *Don't I need any of this stuff anymore?*

Then there are the pain meds. I love my little pump, but I have to be honest, I am not feeling much pain. Maybe that's because the meds are working. Maybe if they take me off of all this stuff, I will be in excruciating pain? But I have to trust my doctors. They know what is best and when I am ready and when I am not. Certainly, I'm not the first guy to have this surgery. Hell, they've probably done hundreds of these.

Maybe going home three days after surgery is typical. Routine. I can't help it, I just don't trust this idea. I'm looking up at the big goofy smile on Dr. Nelson's face, and I trust him even less. I've read horror stories about doctors sending patients home too early because the insurance companies incentivize them to do so. Is that uber cynical? Maybe so, but I wouldn't be surprised.

"Seems a little soon after surgery doc, no?"

"You'll get better quicker in your own bed, eating your wife's home cooked meals." He glances at Nancy, his big goofy smile getting even bigger and goofier.

She sees the eye contact as an opportunity to start asking questions.

"Does he need to be on a specific diet? Like what does he have to avoid and what is best for him to eat. It seems like they will let him eat anything off the menu here so I was just curious."

Nancy glances at me as if to say *I'm taking charge if you're going home*.

"What do you like to eat? Pizza? Eat pizza. Bacon cheeseburger? Eat a bacon cheeseburger. Eat what you like and get your strength back. It's more important to focus on getting up and moving as much as you can. The blood circulating throughout your body will make it heal faster."

Right after I found out I had cancer, I got really strict about eating healthy. I bought into Russ's liquid weeds therapy. Tried to avoid wheat and other things that would spike my blood sugar. Lost some weight. Now this medical professional is telling me to eat pizza and bacon cheeseburgers. The already low trust level continues to sink even lower.

"So it sounds like you want me to trade my cancer for a freaking heart attack."

"I'm just telling you that your surgery is over. We got the cancer, and you aren't required to restrict your diet in any way. Eat what you normally eat."

Apparently having enough of my humor, Dr. Nelson starts to shuffle his way toward the door.

"I'll come in tomorrow and check on you but unless you suffer some sort of setback, which you won't, you're ready to spring this joint. You can thank me tomorrow. Have a good night buddy."

Nancy looks at me and rolls her eyes. I can see the nervousness in her face, and I try to set her mind at ease.

"If I don't feel ready to go home tomorrow I will tell them that I am staying. I'm not going to dump this burden on you until I am comfortable getting up and around on my own. I don't give a shit what Dr. Bozo says."

"He's a weird guy. Kind of rough around the edges. I didn't like the way he pulled that bandage off of you. He was way too rough. I almost said something. And was he serious about you eating pizza? How can a doctor tell someone that? I wish Dr. Matthews were here."

"Yeah, well don't worry about it. I might be laid up in this bed, but they can't force me to leave. We'll see how it goes tomorrow. Why don't you go home and get some sleep? Whoever the night nurse is will give me my medicine and that kind of knocks me out anyway. You look tired."

"Don't worry about me, I'm fine. Russ has been calling me wanting to know when he can come up. What do you want me to tell him?"

"Tell him what they said about me going home and tell him that if I feel up to it, he can come up next week. No sense in him coming to the hospital if they are talking about sending me home."

Nancy isn't relaxed. I can see the tension in her body language and her face. I can tell the idea of me going home tomorrow worries her, as it does me. I meant what I said. I'll put up a fight if I don't think I should be going home. Even if I feel well enough, I don't want her to have to be bothered with taking care of me on top of everything she has to do for her mom every day. Despite my circumstances, I am starting to feel strong right now. I like it.

As I lie here alone in my room with only the faint dim of light protruding from under the door, I start thinking about this next phase. Over the past 2 months, I have focused almost exclusively on the surgery and prognosis. I realize that I've not really thought about post-surgery issues like what it would be like to be home recovering. I'm a little anxious because I feel like I failed to prepare for this part of the process. I think about how Nan recovered so much more quickly than expected after her hip replacements and think that maybe Dr. Nelson might actually be right on this. My thoughts are clearer right now than they have been in a long time. I start to open my mind to the possibility that I can get out of this hospital and this time tomorrow night I will be in my own bed, use my own bathroom and be surrounded by familiar things. Getting up and down today was easier than I thought. I've had enough of all of these contraptions and bags of fluid that I am connected to. Ok, maybe this isn't such a bad idea after all.

It's 9:10. I'll give myself a little pump of pain medicine magic and drift off to sleep. Tomorrow is a big day.

November 30th 2012
7:25 a.m.

"Good morning Mr. Dan, I am Angel". Ah, my day nurse. She is flashing a big smile as she rolls the big medicine cart up to the side of my bed. I have been awake since about 6:30 and feeling more normal than I have since I got here. I'd say about 80% improvement over how I felt, this time, yesterday.

"Angel! What a perfect name for a nurse! What do you have in store for me today? Don't say dancing because you'll be very disappointed."

Angel lets out a hardy laugh, and I think *hey, finally somebody who laughs at my stupid jokes!* I look over at all of the stuff on the medicine tray. Pretty typical of what I've seen the last couple of days. Syringes, a little paper cup with pills in it.

"Ok, no dancing today. Maybe tomorrow. Today we'll just go for a walk. How's the pain this morning?"

Every time they ask me this question I feel the need to really think about it and give as accurate an answer as possible. I focus on my body, particularly the incision area. I can't say I feel pain, but I feel very bloated. My midsection is uncomfortable, almost like my belly is pushing up on my lungs. How do I describe this?

"I'd say the pain is about a 3 but I feel really bloated right now, and that is making me kind of uncomfortable."

"Ok, have you been using the toilet?"

Using the toilet? I so want to come up with a smart ass response to that, but she has asked it in such a serious way I decide against it.

"I pretty much slept through the night so not really."

"The bloating is probably gas. Do you need to use the bathroom now?"

As she is inquiring about my bathroom needs, Angel is peeling back my gown exposing my right leg. That's odd. I am shaking my head in the negative to answer her last question, but she is not looking at me. She has a little wad of gauze that she is rubbing on the top of my thigh. The smell of alcohol is unmistakable, and I immediately connect the dots.

"WHAT'S THIS ABOUT ANGEL?" I'm sure my voice reflected my fear.

"This is your Lovenox injection. No big deal."

I see the needle, and my whole body tenses up.

"I gotta tell you I really hate needles, Angel. Yesterday the nurse gave me a good dose of pain medication before she gave me the shot and I think it helped. Can we wait on this for a while?"

Angel's face crinkles up a bit as if to fain concern. She doesn't stop prepping the needle though, and I try to turn away.

"Just hit your pump. This will be nothing. Trust me."

She's going to do this. A strange sense of resolve comes over me. It's like a different part of me is fighting away the fear. *I've experienced this before, and it wasn't that bad. I can handle this.* I close my eyes and hit the button on my pain pump. A second later I feel a quick tinge of pressure accompanied by a slight sting at the top of my thigh.

"See that? A piece of cake and now you can go about your day, Dan."

I still feel the sting and try to gather my emotions. Needles have always caused me so much anxiety, but right now I am beginning to think I might be overcoming my phobia. A weird sense of pride comes over me. I'm ready to chat with Angel now.

"They still talking about me going home today?"

"I'll ask the doctor and let you know. That would be exciting right? I'm sure you're ready to get out of here." Angel is multi-tasking. She sticks a clamp on my finger, and I hear the familiar sound of Velcro separating on the blood pressure machine.

"I guess so, but I'm not so sure my wife would agree," I say as I glance over at all of the stuff on hanging off of the metal tree that I am hooked up to.

"So if I go home today, I don't need any of this stuff that you have plugged into me? Seems kind of drastic." *If I ain't gonna need it at home, why can't we get rid of it now?* I think to myself.

"The doctor won't send you home until he is sure you are ready. You're doing great, though. All your vitals are good. You're eating well, and I see you've been able to get up. I won't be at all surprised if you end up sleeping in your own bed tonight."

'*Eating well'? ...Able to get up'? How does my new friend Angel know this?* I guess they track this stuff.

"Let's get up and walk some. It's important that you get up as much as possible because it promotes healing."

Angel lowers the railing on the bed and moves into position to help me up. For the first time, I have total confidence that I can get up on my own so I pull my feet up and start maneuvering out of the bed. My feet gently land on the floor, and I push myself into a standing position. The blood rushes to my head, but I feel steady. The hospital socks with the little rubber nubs on the bottom shuffle under my feet as I start to walk.

"Super!" says Angel as she grasps my elbow. "Do you feel like walking out into the hall? I'll stay with you, and you can walk as much or as little as you'd like, but try to do as much as you can. Are you ok?"

"Yup. We might end up dancing after all Angel." I feel pretty good except for the bloaty feeling in my stomach. I sense that I am slouching a bit so I try to straighten up and stand as tall as possible. While the stretching in my back feels pretty good, I can feel the strain across my abdomen which is uncomfortable. I decide that slouching isn't such a bad thing, and I will wait until the incisions heal a bit more before I return to my full upright position.

It smells differently in the hall. Fresher in some ways, more medicinal in others. I just like that it is different. It's brighter too, and I welcome the change of scenery. I feel stronger and more confident than I have since I got here.

The idea of going home suddenly becomes a strong desire. I'm walking and have virtually no pain. My head is clear, and I can tell that I have come a long way just since yesterday. I can't wait to show Nancy how well I'm doing and tell her that I am ready to go home.

"You're doing great Dan. Let me know if you feel dizzy or tired, and we will head back."

I subtly pull my arm away from Angel's grasp and take hold of a railing along the wall. I want to do this on my own. I am guiding the rolling tree with all of the stuff hanging off of it as I walk. My confidence builds with every step. I am feeling stronger not weaker as I walk. I set my sights on a lounge area with a big window that is at the end of the sterile hallway. *Let's see what that view looks like*. I pick up speed a bit and check to see if I am feeling dizzy or tired. Nope. Just a little winded. Jeez, it feels like somebody pumped up my stomach with a tire hose. The lounge is 10 feet away, and I can see that the floor to ceiling window overlooks a pond with some greenery around it. Nice. Everything seems so open compared to my hospital room. Everything seems more normal. I long for normal again, and this is my first indication that I might actually experience it soon. The last 10 minutes have totally changed my perspective, and I am excited. *Things are looking up. Things are getting better.* I feel a smile come across my face. I wish Nancy were here.

"Can I call my wife when we get back to the room?"

"Of course! Does she know that you might be going home today?"

I think back to last night. I could see the concern in her eyes about my going home and resolved not to put her through it. This morning everything has changed. I want to tell her that

I've got this, and she doesn't need to worry. Patience is not one of my better virtues, and I WANT TO TELL HER NOW!

"We talked about it last night, but we weren't sure it was such a good idea. I feel a lot better today, and I really want to let her know that if I do go home today, she doesn't have to worry."

"Let's go back and call her!" Angel has a sincere smile. I like her even though she recently impaled my skin. She's positive, and I am all about positive right now. I pivot and start walking back to the room. I am standing up straighter and taller. I'm winning. I like this feeling.

"I should be there in 15 minutes." Nancy still sounds apprehensive as she tells me this. It will be better to speak with her face to face anyway. I am back in bed and wish I had stayed up, walking with Angel so that she could have seen me but she will see enough of me soon.

"Ok, well I'm back in bed, but I feel like I'm doing pretty well. See you when you get here."

"Love you." Even in a 2-second conversation, my wife tells me she loves me. Maybe it is just a reflex closing to our phone calls, but I like hearing it anyway. More now than ever.

"Love you too."

I feel more alive than I have in quite a while. A million thoughts are racing through my head about this day. Realizing that I have enjoyed the luxury of having a button that moves my bed into whatever angle I desire to make me comfortable, I wonder how I'll do in my regular bed at home? *Maybe propping up pillows will be just as good?* Thinking about home makes me happy. Like so many things that I have reflected on through this ordeal, I know I will appreciate my home more than ever now. It is so easy to take the things around you for granted every day. The beauty and comfort of your home almost becomes invisible because you are immersed in it for so much of your life, but it is such a blessing. I promise myself at that moment that the minute I step into our beautiful home, I will take it all in. I will appreciate everything I see. I'm going to look more closely at every detail… the furniture, the pictures that hold such great memories, the features that Nancy and I designed into our dream house. I will look more closely at everything, and I will embrace the happiness that it all brings. I will be grateful, and I will try to tap into that gratitude every day for the rest of my life, no matter how long that may be.

I'm hungry. I think this is the first time since surgery that I have actually felt hungry. *Another positive sign that things are getting back to normal.* My confidence is building by the minute. *I'll enjoy a nice breakfast this morning, Nan will see how well I am doing and then I will head home.*

Nancy and my breakfast arrive at the same time. I can smell the eggs under the metal cover, and my hunger pangs get stronger. After a quick morning greeting, Nan gets right to the point.

"Has the doctor been in yet? Are they still talking about you going home today?" I try to read her eyes to see any sign of whether she is asking this from a positive or negative point of view. My wife's face is radiant as usual, but she looks tired. I can see the stress, and I want to take it off of her.

"Haven't seen the doc yet, but I walked all over this floor earlier. I can get up pretty much on my own, and I am actually hungry. No pain meds necessary this morning. If they want to send me home, I think it will be fine."

"You walked all over the floor? That's awesome honey! Did someone help you? Please tell me you didn't try this on your own." Despite the enthusiasm, I can see Nancy's wheels spinning. She is processing the fact that I am making progress. She is probably wondering how much help I am going to need when I get home.

"My new friend Angel walked with me. I did fine. She basically just pushed the stupid IV rack while I walked. It felt great. We went all the way to the end of the hall and back. I'm way better today, and I feel like maybe I turned the corner. I'm ready to go home." I try to muster as much confidence in my voice as possible, and I am waiting for Nancy's reaction.

"Well let's see what the doctor says. I wonder who it will be today?"

Nancy is maneuvering the tray that holds my breakfast over the bed and removing all of the coverings. The eggs look great, and I can feel the heat coming off of them. Maybe this will be the last of the hospital food for me? I start with the apple juice and take a few bites of the eggs. Almost instantly I feel full and hungry at the same time. Weird. I look down at my belly, and it looks bulbous like I swallowed a beach ball. It must be swelling from the surgery. A few more bites of eggs, half the toast and I am done. I've eaten about a third of what is on the tray and the thought of another bite makes me nauseous. *So much for being hungry*.

Dr. Nelson knows how to make an entrance. He is in full scrubs with the surgical mask dangling from his neck. He has a matching surgical beanie on, but his tussled black hair is protruding out from around the edges.

"Hey, hot shot, how ya feeling?" '*Hot shot'?* I guess he has a different name for me each day.

"Much better today doc. I've been up, walked all the way to the end of the hall and scarfed down a nice breakfast. It's been a busy day already. So.... You planning to spring me from this joint today or what?" I figured I'd engage him in the overzealous banter that he seems to enjoy. I think I am up to it today.

"Sounds like you're ready to get out of here. Are you moving your bowels?"

I have to actually think about the question. I know it is the clinically correct way to ask it, but I can't help finding the humor in the wording. *Moving my bowels.* Sounds like manual labor. Why didn't he just say *'Hey did ya poop?'*

"Not too much. I tried but no luck. I can't say I am really looking forward to that first big one if you know what I mean."

Dr. Nelson isn't listening to me. He has his stethoscope out and is listening to my belly. I look down once again and can't help but think I almost look pregnant. The small incision areas look better, and I can see the surgical staples.

I have a tinge of fear as I think about the day when I will have the staples removed. I remember how tough it was when Nan had her staples removed after hip replacement surgery. Hopefully it won't be as bad, but either way, I don't want to focus on that now. *Be in the moment. Right now, I have no pain, and I feel pretty alert.*

"Yeah, you don't need to be in here anymore. You'll do much better at home eating your wife's cooking and sleeping in your own bed. We've got you down for a follow up at our office on Wednesday. Just keep moving and you'll be back to normal before you know it."

I can tell he is getting ready to leave the room, and I realize he hasn't even acknowledged Nancy. She thanks him, and he still doesn't even make eye contact. He pulls the door shut to my room as he walks out and I look up at Nancy. She takes a deep breath, almost a sigh.

"So I wonder what we do now? I think I will go ask the nurse when you will be discharged. Are they going to disconnect all of this stuff?" She is looking inquisitively at the rack that holds all of the fluids and machinery that I am tethered to. I can tell she is concerned but determined and the reality of leaving the hospital sets in for both of us. Going home creates that feeling of uncertainty. *Am I really ready?*

Angel and Nancy become fast friends, and I love the sound of my wife's laughter. I'm not really focused on what they are talking about, I just like the fact that it is happy and jovial. I think about the months before when there was really nothing to laugh about.

Sure, I tried to keep a happy face through it all, but facing cancer and everything that that word means is about as serious as it gets. I want to believe that from this point on, there will be many more happy times, much more laughter, and all of it will be sincere.

The worry of the past couple of months has almost smothered me like a blanket, and as I reflect back on it, I feel the toll that it has taken on me. I am emotionally tired. I welcome the idea of putting that feeling behind me, and I embrace the hope for my second chance. I close my eyes and focus hard on that feeling of hope and optimism. I have a burning desire to recover and get back to enjoying my life. I will appreciate my blessings more than ever, I already know that. I just want the chance.

As much as I find all of the tubes, wires and nodes attached to my body unnerving, the thought of what it might feel like for them to be removed scares me. Especially the needle from this port in my chest. I've never thought about whether or not a needle hurts as much coming out of your skin as it does going into your skin. I can't imagine it would, but I am about to find out. They told me that I will be out of here in about an hour.

A new nurse comes in with a cart full of the typical unidentifiable items on it. She is wearing a surgical mask and those Playtex gloves that tell you she is going to do something that requires such a high level of sanitary protection, that she can't even take a chance on having it touch her skin. Swell.

“I’m here to get you ready to go home. How does that sound?”

I can tell she is smiling under the mask so I try to smile back.

“Are you the unplugging nurse?”

“Well you certainly wouldn’t want to take all of this home with you, would you?”

She has already started playing with the tubes on the rack. She unties the string around the top of my gown and removes the heavy box from the pocket. This is the first I have actually seen the heart monitor. Nothing spectacular, just a black box with wires sticking out of it.

“Oh, you’re a hairy one,” says Nurse No Name as she unclips the nodes that are stuck to my chest. Several have fallen off by themselves, and I wonder why it didn’t make the heart monitor go off or otherwise tell someone that things were amiss? It doesn’t matter now, I am just happy to be rid of this thing.

Surprisingly, the tape surrounding my port comes off easily. I feel the nurse’s fingers against my shoulder and a slight tugging around the port. I figure it was more tape, but when I look up, she is rolling up the tube with a needle attached and putting it into a plastic container with a very ominous looking symbol on it.

I look down and realize that I am untethered for the first time since I got here.

"You can go ahead and get dressed now. Have a great day and be well."

The nurse rolls the rack that holds the fluids and tubes off to the corner of the room and saunters out the door. I sigh loudly and enjoy this moment. *'Another step toward normalcy',* I tell myself.

Nancy has brought me some loose clothes to wear and I am very much looking forward to getting out of this sadomasochistic hospital gown that has been pretending to cover my body for the past 4 days. I don't even know why they call it a gown. "Gown" is an elegant word, not meant for a man. This thing is more like an apron, and not a very well made apron at that. No matter what movement you make in bed the thing wraps around you in exactly the places that it shouldn't. Anyway, my hospital door is open and if I am going to change I either need to close it or go into the bathroom. Since the bathroom is the size of a phone booth, I pull myself out of bed and shuffle close enough to the door to push it shut. I look into the bag that holds the clothes. Grey sweat pants and an oversized sweatshirt. *It must be cold outside.* I haven't even thought about the weather. There are so many things that get suspended in time while you go through something like this. Time itself changes, especially for me. Watching the hours go so slowly. Sleeping when I should be awake. Wide awake when I should be sleeping. Things that I was focused on as a matter of routine have no significance when you are bound to a hospital bed. The weather doesn't matter because there is nowhere I can go. I haven't looked at my phone since I got here. No emails. No calls. No to-do lists. *Are they really as important as I treat them in my day to day life?* For a second I panic, wondering what I might have missed over the past few days. Nothing comes to mind, and I quickly dismiss my panic as unimportant. During the time since I was diagnosed, I have had an awakening about what is important in this life. I have given tremendous amounts of thought to what should be allowed to occupy my precious time each day. This has not been easy. Old habits are hard to break. Still, I have been able to identify the things that are truly important to me and force myself to let go of things that don't have significant meaning. It is a constant process of evaluation…. Minute by minute, day by day. Doing so has a cleansing effect on my mind and my spirit. I actually feel almost enlightened by it. It's a good thing, and I want to be sure to sustain it for the rest of my life, however long that may be. Hell, all of that worry over the unimportant may be part of the reason I got cancer.

I go to reach behind my back and untie the gown only to realize that there is nothing to untie. I guess the nurse took care of that little task for me. A slight tip forward of my torso and the stupid thing slides right down my arms. I feel a chill come over me as the air hits my skin so I quickly grab the sweatshirt and gingerly slide it over my head and shoulders. It feels great.

There is a pair of boxers, but I sense that my very tender midsection might not be too fond of the elastic, so I just put on the baggy sweat pants. This is a bit of a chore, and even the loose waistband hurts the area where my incisions are. I'm tired from this and turn toward the bed only to feel stinging pain across my belly and abdomen. I do not like this and wonder if this is going to be tougher than I thought. My butt hits the bed, and I just sit there. I'm holding the waist line away from my body and decide that it's time to get back into bed until Nancy arrives.

As I gaze out the window, it seems that the sun is starting to set. 4:40. *Where did this day go?* I have been in this state of anticipation all day, and now I start to wonder if they will still let me go home today.

"Yea, you're dressed"! Nancy bounces into the room, and she is all smiles.

"The nurse is getting you a wheelchair and the car is with the valet. Are you ok? You look tired."

I tell her about the discomfort of the baggy sweat pants.

"I brought your robe. Why don't you take those off and just wear the robe. It'll be fine." I'm not sure I want to leave the hospital going "commando" so I opt to tough it out with the sweat pants. Nancy helps me put on a fresh pair of booties and then the robe. By the time we manage all of that, a young man in scrubs shows up with the wheelchair.

I take a quick look around the room. I won't miss it. I'm glad for the care I received here, but it's time to go home. I turn around, and the young man in scrubs takes my arm to help me lower myself into the wheelchair. I'm getting used to the sweatpants and sitting in this hospital version of a chariot I feel pretty comfortable.

We are rolling down the hallway, and I enjoy taking in the sights from a different perspective. As the big double doors open to the elevator lobby, I read the sign on the wall… SURGICAL PCU. I see people coming and going and deduce that they are no doubt there to visit loved ones who are recovering from surgery in rooms like the one I just left. This floor is a mix of pain and comfort. I am leaving this place feeling positive and optimistic. Many of the faces I see show the fear and concern that permeated my life just a few days ago. I quietly hope for positive outcomes for all of those on this floor. I think about the loved ones whom I see getting off the elevator and walking toward the people in those rooms, knowing that they are most likely going to see them suffering in many ways, physically and emotionally. I hope that all of them will be leaving here soon with the same feeling of positivity that I have right now and that the loved ones who are here supporting them will feel the relief that I hope Nancy is feeling right now as she takes me back home. The elevator door closes, and I feel a gentle jolt as we descend from the 14th floor. Even though it has only been 4 days, this seems like a whole new experience. As the doors open, there is lively activity all around. The hospital is crowded, and I don't remember it being this big. The day's last bit of sunlight is streaming through the glass doors ahead, and I see Nancy's car in front.

"It's a little chilly out." She says as she moves ahead of us to get to the car door.

The smell of the cool fresh air is energizing, and I take a long deep breath. I am alive. I am recovering, and I am going home. I close my eyes and feel the gratitude for this moment. When I open my eyes, the car door is wide open, and Nancy is lifting my feet off of the wheel chair platform. She and the orderly are on either side of me and seem to be trying to figure out how to stand me up.

"I got it," I said as I pushed myself up to a vertical position. I'm a little weak in the knees, and I feel out of breath, but I shuffle toward the car and start the slow process of folding myself into the passenger seat. I haven't twisted and turned too much, and I can really feel it. Twinges of pain are hitting me from numerous angles across my mid-section, but I keep adjusting until I lower myself into the car. The orderly lifts my feet up and maneuvers my legs into the car, smiles and closes the door. I made it. As Nancy gets into her side, she looks at me with a very serious face.

"Are you ok? Are you in pain?"

"I'm freaking great. Let's go home." I say trying to muster a smile.

The ride home is not the most enjoyable as I feel every single bump and turn rip across my belly. My knuckles are white from bracing myself against every natural movement the car makes. It seemed to take forever but we finally arrive, and the house never looked so good to me.

"Wait here. I am going to get the walker, and that will make it easier for you to get into the house." She says. Anxiety is building. I don't need the damn walker, and I want to get into the house.

Billy emerges from the front door, and I am thrilled to see him. He watches Nancy scurry inside but comes out to open the door for me with his typical greeting … "hey…"

"You doing good? You look good." Billy is a man of few words but has the biggest heart in the universe. He gives me energy, and I start getting out of the car. He wants to try and help me out but seems not to know how. He grabs my elbow and about that time Nancy arrives with the walker. This is the same walker she used when she was recovering from hip replacement surgery. I have to admit, having it to lean on made the walk inside much easier.

By the time I reached the bedroom, Nancy and Billy had already turned the covers down and placed a wedge pillow against the head board to prop me up. Perfect.

I stop to look around my house and soak in the comfort of its familiarity. It seems like a long time since I have been here but I know it hasn't. The person who left here on Tuesday had a cancerous tumor in his body. That person was fearful and gloomy. Today I am recovering from the removal of that tumor and feeling very upbeat. My job now is to recover from this and fulfill the promises I made to myself over the past couple of months. I will be a better person. I will fight to beat this, and I will win. I have a lot of living to do, and it starts here, in my home, surrounded by the people that I live for.

The bed looks good to me, and I realize the toll this day has taken. I'm whipped. The annoying sweat pants come off, and I lower myself into my bed wearing my robe and the sweatshirt. Nancy swings my legs up into the bed and the comfort I feel as the bed envelopes my body is indescribable.

Billy is lingering near the door, and Nancy is playing nurse.

“Are you hungry? I bought soup.” She says as she places a cup of water by the bed.

“I just want to lay here for a while. I’m bushed. Plus, I feel kind of bloated and out of breath. I’m good for now. Just really glad to be home with you guys.”

“Ok, well let me know. You need to eat so that you get your strength back. Wanna watch tv?”

“I’m fine. I just want to lay here. So what’s up?” I direct my attention to Billy.

“Nothing much.’ As I said, Billy is a man of few words. “Let me know if you want me to get you anything.”

I suddenly feel like all of my energy is leaving my body. My stomach is puffy and tight, my back is aching, and I feel like I could go right to sleep. I want to enjoy these moments, but I am so tired. I look at the clock, and it says 7:05. I should probably try to start getting back into a regular sleep pattern. I don’t have the Dilaudid to knock me out so I have to fall asleep naturally.

Almost on cue as I think of this, Nancy asks me if I want a pain pill.

Yes, indeed I do want a pain pill. I can't quite pinpoint where I feel pain, but I know I need a pain pill. I have a fleeting thought that this might mean I am becoming addicted, but I doubt that is possible after only a few days. She digs into the plastic bag that she brought with her from the hospital and takes out a prescription bottle. She rattles one out and puts it in my hand, simultaneously handing me the cup of water. It goes down easy, and I feel the cool liquid going down my throat. Even though I know it will take a while for it to kick in, I feel better knowing I took it.

I close my eyes and reflect on the moment. I'm home. I am recovering, and I commit to being smart about it. It is the only thing that matters to me right now. First order of business...sleep.

December 1st, 2012

It was a pretty restful night, but I wake up feeling a bit sickly. It is hard to put my finger on specific symptoms, but I just feel shitty. My belly seems so bloated that it is making me uncomfortable, and I have wicked indigestion. I assume this is my body starting to adjust to life after surgery, and I tell myself it must be part of the process. I lay in bed taking in my new surroundings. The daylight permeating my bedroom gives me a nice feeling of serenity, and I let my body relax. Nowhere to go today. No responsibilities. Nothing really to do other than let myself get better. I hear Nancy in the kitchen rattling dishes and utensils around. She doesn't know I am awake, and I decide to just lay here resting until she comes in to check on me. When that happens is unimportant. I view time differently now. Every moment is meaningful and precious, even if that moment consists of simply laying comfortably in my bed, staring at the ceiling and contemplating my thoughts. I like this, and it feels right.

I glance down at my midsection. *Holy crap, I look pregnant!* I wonder why I am so damn bloated? Maybe I ate too much yesterday? Maybe my body is having trouble digesting solid foods? I hope this bloated belly isn't stretching my incisions. I catch myself worrying and try my best to let it go. *They wouldn't have let me go home if something was wrong.* I try to take a deep breath, but it is a bit of a struggle. I am a little short of breath, but I guess that is to be expected.

Nancy gently opens our bedroom door and walks toward me.

"Hey, sleeping beauty is awake!"

I have a beautiful wife. She is beautiful both inside and out, but she is particularly attractive to me in the morning. She would not agree with me because she is very conscientious about her appearance, always wanting to look her best. But to me, the sight of her smiling as she walks toward me, the sound of her happy voice… it just pleases me to no end.

"You must have slept well because you were snoring like a freaking bear. Are you hungry? Do you want to get up or do you want me to bring something in here for you? I could make you some eggs. Does that sound good to you?"

Not sure which question to answer first, I just tell her that I am fine and ask her to sit next to me on the bed. I tell her about my bloaty feeling and that I look pregnant.

"Your body has been through a lot of trauma, and I am sure there is swelling down there." She says.

"Thank you, Nurse Nancy, but it doesn't feel or look like swelling. I feel like I ate a basketball and my stomach is churning. Maybe I will eat something a little later, but for now, I think I will just have some water."

Nancy springs into action and fetches me a bottle of water. I take a few gulps, but I don't like the way it feels going down my throat and into my stomach. It just doesn't feel right for some reason. Maybe I need to get up and try to walk around some.

"I'm going to get up" I proclaim like it should be broadcast to the media. Nancy takes this as her cue to fetch the walker for me. As I pull back the covers and carefully maneuver my legs off the bed and my feet onto the floor, I sense a rush of blood to my head and it makes me a bit woozy. As I push myself to a seated position, I take a moment to brace for the potential pain of standing on my own. *I'm doing this. I'm going to push this recovery and get back to normal as fast as I can.* As I have experienced several times throughout this recovery, the standing and walking I thought would be so tough were really nothing at all. I used the walker that Nancy brought me but only because I didn't want her to feel that she wasted the effort. I could have walked to the bathroom on my own.

Damn, my belly is fat! I try to ignore the weirdness around my puffed up midsection and go about my day. At first, it seems awkward walking around my house. It shouldn't… I wasn't gone that long, but in many ways, I came home a different person. Maybe that is part of the adjustment. The familiarity feels good, but it is taking me a while to adjust to my surroundings in the condition that I am in. It has been only 4 days since my surgery, and I have mixed emotions. On one hand, I feel like I should be in worse shape after only 4 days. Not home walking around. On the other hand, I honestly feel like shit right now. No real pain, I just feel sickly. I guess this is what recovery feels like. I've been up for all of 45 minutes, and I am ready to go back to bed. Ugh.

I've been dozing for most of the day. I recall Nancy telling me that she was going to her mom's which tells me it is around 3:00 or so. Everything is quiet, the bedroom is dim, and I am just lying on my back staring at nothing in particular. In these first quite moments I've had since coming home, I start assessing where I've been, where I am and what might be next. I am not feeling healthy and for some reason I am fearful. Anxiety has always been one of my major demons, but this is just fear. I think when you have doubts about having a future, fear simply permeates your being. The future is always something I talk about. It is pretty much always on my mind. The future of my career. Hell, I'm 55, and I am still thinking about the future and my career. Retirement, whatever that is and whether I will ever be able to afford to do it. Now, the future of my physical abilities. Five days ago I had a cancerous tumor in my gut, but I felt fine and could do just about anything I wanted. Now the tumor is gone but what does that mean for my future? Did they get it all? If not, what's next? What the hell is chemo going to be like? God, I've heard so many horror stories. How am I going to deal with it? When do I get declared as "cured," if I should be so lucky? I've always heard five years. Damn that is a long time. I'll be 60! Will I be able to function once this recovery is over? The questions rattle around in my head like a pinball, and I feel the emotions welling up inside me. I've cried more in the past ten weeks than I have the rest of my life combined. Crying is not a sign of weakness or a negative implication of your manhood. It is a natural emotional reaction. I don't burst into tears, but I have that lump in my throat and the welling up of water in my eyes. *I hate the unknown….it makes me feel so out of control.* I wish I could just go back to sleep and wake up feeling better. Maybe I could take a pill? *What time did I take that last pain pill? 2:00?* Can't do that. I guess I just have to try and let it go. '*Live in the moment. There are going to be times like these, but everything is going to be ok'* I tell myself. I'm not sure I believe it.

Complications

December 2nd, 2012
3:10 a.m.

I'm sick. Something is wrong. I am not sure what. Without much thought, I lumber myself out of bed and waddle to the bathroom. I'm not even sure if I have to go to the bathroom, but something tells me to get in there. It is a long walk….my stomach is so bloated I can hardly breathe. I feel pressure as far up as my throat. As I sit on the throne, I experience a very unnatural purge that just isn't right. Details are not something you want to read, but it is not pretty. I am confused. *Is this supposed to be this way or is something wrong?* I don't want to wake Nancy up, but I really feel the need to do so. I'm in such distress that I can't even open my mouth to call her name. Luckily, I don't have to.

"Everything all right?" I hear from the other room. All I can muster is "No, it's not" and I hope I was able to say it loud enough for her to hear me through the bathroom door.

Her voice is right in front of me now, and I hear the concern. "What's the matter?" The half closed door slowly swings open, and I see her silhouette in front of me. It hurts to lift my head. I am starting to feel nauseous, and I am trying to open my mouth to tell Nancy that something is wrong with me.

"I just feel so sick. I am burning up and feel nauseous. I just had some sort of explosion come out of me and my stomach feels like it is going to burst." There. I think that covers it for now.

I decide I don't want to sit anymore and push myself up off the toilet. Everything feels stiff and achy. When I get upright, the nausea increases. *I have to get back to the bed.* Every step makes me feel worse and more feverish. I am facing the realization that this is definitely not part of my recovery process. This is BAD.

"Maybe you should drink some water and get back into bed. Do you want me to call the doctor?" The idea of swallowing anything, including water makes me more nauseous. I see the bottle of water next to the bed, and as I sit down, decide that maybe Nancy knows best. She opens the bottle, and I take some very tentative sips. This is not making me feel better.

"Call the doctor. I'll talk to him" I say without really even thinking about it. My instincts tell me that this is the right call.

Nancy seems to panic a little as she looks for Dr. Matthews's number and reaches for her cell phone. Of course, she gets the service, and the doc on call has to call us back. More waiting and if there was ever a time when I did not want to wait, it is now. I seem to be feeling worse by the second. A wave of cold sweat pours over me, and my belly is about to burst. My guts seem to be in my throat, and I am fighting the urge to throw up.

I am holding Nancy's cell and answer immediately when it rings.

"Hello, this is Doctor Kiresh."

I set my increasing discomfort aside and carefully explain what I am feeling to the very sleepy sounding doctor on the other end of my wife's cell phone. I feel my hand start to tremble.

"Drink some water and try to rest. It is probably just your body adjusting to the solid foods. If it isn't better in the morning, make an appointment to come in and we'll check it out."

"Doc I really feel awful. Are you sure I don't need to get back to the hospital?"

"Are you vomiting?"

"No, but I am really nauseous. I feel like I could."

"Try to rest. If you need to go back to the hospital, you will know."

I didn't like the conversation. I didn't like his accent. I didn't like how calm he was. He did not seem concerned, and while that should probably give me some comfort, it just frustrated me.

I take another sip of the water and now I really do feel like I am going to puke. I am fighting it, but I feel it coming.

"I'm going to throw up," I announce to Nancy. Simultaneously I am headed for the bathroom to deposit what I know is coming into the proper receptacle. Three steps toward the bathroom and I feel it coming up. *I'm not going to make it.*

The next five minutes seems like an eternity. I am vomiting violently, and it is sapping all of my strength. My knees are Jello, and my head is pounding. I feel like my body temperature is 212 degrees and there are tears rolling down my face. Whatever is projecting out of my body is utterly horrible. When a brief moment of relief comes, I try to stand.

I see Nancy's face, and it is contorted with helpless fear. She's saying something to me, but I cannot focus on what it is.

"Call an ambulance and get me back to the hospital." This was not an instruction that I needed to think about. I need medical attention, and I need it NOW. Fuck Dr. Kiresh and his "drink water and rest" bullshit. I feel like my body is being ripped inside out, and I could ignite at any moment. I make it back into the bed and for a fleeting moment try to remember if I had ever felt as bad as I do at this moment. *Not even close.*

I hear Nancy talking to the 911 operator and relaying my information as well as the hospital location. She isn't on long and turns to see me barfing into the towels and buckets which she has positioned around the bed. Thank God for my wonderful wife.

"I am calling the Doctor back to tell him we are headed to the hospital." She informs me. She has taken charge. I know she doesn't like it, but my wife rises to the occasion when she needs to.

The vomiting is getting more violent, and I feel my guts straining as I heave. *This is definitely going to cause me to bust a stitch.* I have no strength left now. The vomiting has become a very unpleasant reflex that I have no control over. It isn't stopping. I am getting light headed and think I might pass out.

In a matter of minutes, I open my eyes to see three men in EMT uniforms walking into my house and a large stretcher which they somehow get through the front door. The unmistakable flashing lights of their emergency vehicle are dancing around my house, and the thought occurs to me that they are probably waking up my neighbors. I could give a shit less.

Nancy is answering some of their basic questions, and one of the guys is taking my vital signs. I know I am going to puke again, and I try to warn him by pulling the soaked towel up to my face. I let go another round of vile and he hands me this weird plastic tube thing with a sack at the end of it. I assume I can vomit into this from now on. Swell.

Somehow I end up on the gurney, and the EMT says they are going to insert an IV into my arm.

“No, you can’t. I have a port. Can you do it through the port?” I am groggy and not quite sure if I am saying the right things.

“No sir, we are not authorized to access a port. They’ll have to do that when we get to the hospital. We can start the IV or wait ‘til we get to the hospital, and they can access the port. What do you want to do?”

You want me to make a fucking decision? In this condition?

“Let’s wait ‘til we are at the hospital. I am in a lot of pain. Can you give me anything?”

“No, sir. They can help you when we get to the hospital.”

My body is being jostled around as the gurney is loaded into the back of the ambulance. I have never been in an ambulance before. It looks like a cargo truck with a bunch of medical crap around the inside. Not really what I had envisioned.

“I’ll be following right behind you.” I hear Nancy’s voice as they close the door to the ambulance. I am still vomiting, and the bumpy ride isn’t helping at all. I want to look around but barely have the strength to lift my head up. This plastic tube is disgusting by now, and I think about asking for a new one. I can't generate the words.

The guys in the ambulance are not saying anything. That's ok with me. I hear a beeping sound and see some machinery with flashing numbers. They must be attached to me somehow. I don't know, and I really don't care right now.

We are pulling into the hospital, and I feel some hope that I can get some relief. There is a clock at the entrance. *4:55*. I've been vomiting for over an hour straight. *Where the hell did all this "stuff" inside me come from? I haven't eaten that much, have I?*

The gurney comes to rest in a bright hallway near a reception area. I see a few people around and two young ladies in scrubs who are paying no attention to me lying there. I puke again and afterward look up. They weren't paying any attention at all.

Maybe I am hallucinating and they aren't even there or maybe I am just imagining that I am puking up my guts. I know that neither is true, but it strikes me odd that no one is paying any attention to me. I need something for the pain, and I want to tell one of these medical stiffs, but I can't conjure up the strength to speak. I try to pinpoint where I have pain. *The pain is everywhere and nowhere. My entire body is toxic.*

I laid my head back on the poor excuse for a pillow and closed my eyes. At that moment I knew I was dying. Every ounce of my being was beginning to rot from the inside out. *This is what it feels like to die.* My heart began to pound, and I felt like I was going to cry again. I tried to focus my thoughts on something else…. Anything else. My surroundings, my family, what might come next, anything. But all I could think about was the total surety that this was the end. *What the hell happened? They sent me home and now this? I've never heard of cancer doing this to a person. Why isn't someone trying to help me?*

I can hear Nancy's voice, but I don't see her. I think about dying with her by my side and it makes me both happy and sad. Happy that she is the last vision I will see and hear, but sad that she will have to experience the moment of my death. She gets the raw end of that deal, and it is selfish for me to think this way.

Thoughts of death have always scared me. I guess that is natural. The fact that everything and everyone goes on but it all stops at the moment of death is an unsettling thought for me. Maybe because I know I won't be able to participate any longer. Maybe I am afraid I will miss something. Strange. What will life be like for my wife and sons when I am no longer around. Is Nancy going to be able to pay for a funeral? I wonder who will be there?

Damn it! I wish I had gotten that fucking life insurance! I've been living my life worried about our finances, and now I am going to die with that worry on my mind. And I won't be here to fix it. The guilt reins over me. I'm overwhelmed with negative thoughts, and the nausea is back. I don't want to be sick anymore. If this is the end, let's just get it over with. I'm suffering and nobody within 30 feet of me gives a shit. This is a hospital and they are supposed to care for the sick. Maybe they see no hope for me so they aren't bothering.

"NAN" I muster the strength to bark my wife's name. The power in my voice surprises me, and I look up to see the medical sorority sisters looking back at me like I just interrupted their coffee talk session. *Fuck you. You're standing there tallking about some brainless TV show while I lie dying 10 feet away.*

"The doctor is on his way, and they are getting ready to put you into a room. Are you feeling any better?" I finally see my wife standing beside my gurney. I want to tell her I am sorry for putting her through all of this, but I can't find the words. Instinctively I want help and relief, so I figure the only way that is going to happen is to speak up to whoever will listen. Right now, the only one who seems willing to do that is my wife.

"Get me something for pain. And something to make this vomiting stop. PLEASE!" I hear Nancy talking to one of the "do nothing" medical ladies at the reception counter, but I don't know what she is saying. I am trying to push these thoughts of death out of my head, but the decaying feeling in my body won't let me.

My senses are dull, and my breathing is weak. There is a cold chill on my neck, and I wonder if it is sweat or somehow the vile crud coming out of me made it back there. It doesn't matter. Something about feeling the onset of death in your body changes the way you think. Right now I only care about my wife and my sons. *My sons.* Panic overtakes me as I realize that I might not see my sons before I die. *I have to hold on until they get here.*

"The doctor will be here any minute, and they are going to get you something for pain. They asked me if you had a "power port." Do you know? They have to get a special nurse to access the port, and they are calling for her. Are you feeling any better at all?" I hear Nancy's questions, but I can't process anything right now. What the hell is a *power port* and why don't THEY know if I have one or not?

"I have no idea. Just get me some help or knock me out or something…" I am babbling. *Do I tell Nancy that I feel like I am dying? I just can't do that. The doctors will tell her. Or it will just become obvious.* She rubs her hand over my head, and it feels very comforting. I focus in on her face and see the fatigue combined with stress, and it makes me very sad. I fear that both will get worse before they get better.

The gurney is moving. I don't see anyone, and Nancy's not there. *Did I doze off?* The sides of the gurney bang against the door jamb as I enter a brightly lit but very small room with medical equipment all around it. A large dark skinned man appears at the foot of the gurney and positions it with the head up against the wall. The glass opening gives me a view into the hallway that I just came from, and I see quite a few more medical personnel scurrying about. *Are they here for me?* I don't recognize anyone that I saw earlier.

The guy who wheeled me into the room leaves and never says a word to me. I am alone in the room now and wondering what happens next. Being left to just lie here alone with a barf bag while doctors and nurses and who knows what other kind of medical professionals occupy all of the space around me…..it just doesn't seem right. It kind of pisses me off. *Is somebody out there going to do something to help me?*

Nancy enters the room with a young nurse. The nurse isn't smiling. I wonder if that is a bad sign or perhaps just the result of having to deal with sick people at 5 in the morning. She wraps the blood pressure cuff around my arm and puts a stethoscope against my stomach. I can't decide which is more annoying.

"Is somebody getting me something for pain?" I ask.

Nancy and the nurse start talking at the same time saying that they are going to put the port in and then start giving me medicine for pain and nausea. I hear them talking about this "power port" issue, and the nurse says something about a CT scan. The voices and sounds are all running together, and I can't focus on any of it. I don't really know what they are saying, and I don't really care. *Is this the room I am going to die in?* I sure as hell hope not. It's cramped, stark and too bright. *Maybe I should have stayed home.*

I close my eyes and try to block everything out, but my mind is spinning out of control. *Has Nancy called the boys? How much longer do I have? Is it going to get worse? I hope there is a heaven. Will I get to see my parents again?* Enough. *Live in the moment.* I tell myself over and over again. I am almost chanting it. Unfortunately, the moment really sucks right now. Nancy's hand grasps mine and I open my eyes.

"They want to do a CT scan to try and figure out what is going on. They keep asking me if your port was a "power port" because that is what you need to have the CT scan. I have no idea what they are talking about, do you?" asks Nancy.

I just shake my head with a grimaced face.

What the hell is that smell? I know it is cologne but, woof! It is followed by loud footsteps and the sound of a deep baritone, heavily accented voice.

"I am doctor Tanadin. Dr. Matthews sent me here to look after you. Tell me what has been going on."

I look down the length of my body to the foot of the gurney. Dr. Tanadin is an unusual looking man. Tall and solid, he is obviously African American, but his skin is pale white. He wears thick glasses and looks like he hasn't laughed since he was five years old. His appearance combined with the pungent cologne makes me uncomfortable, but I force myself to push the judgment from my mind. *He said "Doctor" Tanadin. He must have the power to help me.*

"If you're a doctor then get me something for pain and figure out why I am puking my guts out." I doubt if my voice is very authoritative but I give it my best shot. I see him stare at me as if surprised by what he just heard.

"You haven't been given anything for pain?"

"NURSE. COME HERE. This man is in pain and requires immediate attention. Get me 4 milligrams of Dilaudid and re-engage the port." Dr. Tanadin's voice is loud and intimidating. Suddenly people in scrubs are running all over the place, and one of them comes into the room with some paperwork. Dr. Tanadin nudges him aside with barely a glance and positions himself back at the foot of the gurney. He looks at me and then toward Nancy who is seated by the door.

"I am in charge now, and we are going to get you some relief."

Whoa. That's strong. He barks and people start running. He may not look like Marcus Welby, but he can sure make things happen. Within 90 seconds there are no less than 3 medical people in this little room, one with a big steel cart. She is wearing a surgical mask and latex gloves. The adrenaline must be kicking in because I feel a twinge of energy as I look at all of the activity going on in this little space. Dr. Tanadin seems to tower above all of it looking on. *Yes, he is definitely in charge now.*

A woman's voice is in my ear speaking in almost a whisper.

"I am going to insert the port needle so that we can start fixing you up, ok?"

I want to turn my head to look at her, but I don't have to. I smell her breath through the surgical mask, and she has her hands on my chest. Then I feel the pain.

"AAAAGGGHHH" I know I am yelling. The needle penetrating my skin not only is causing me excruciating pain but feels totally unnatural. It seems to take forever, and I feel every centimeter of the steel sliding through my flesh.

“All done.” Says the nurse as she starts fumbling around with tape and gauze and the like. I feel a tear run down my cheek and my body is uncoiling from the intense pain of the needle. *This is why I hate fucking needles.* Usually, after I get one I can say that it wasn’t as bad as I made it out to be in my mind, but this one sure exceeded my expectations. At least I didn’t have any time to think about it before she plowed it into my chest.

I just want to close my eyes and make this stop. The pain from the injection exhausts me even more than before which I didn't think was possible. My stomach is tight, but I am not feeling quite as nauseous, so maybe I can drift off and things will get better. Any thoughts of peace and quiet are lost when I hear the booming voice of Dr. Tanadin.

"I can give you some good news this morning. I pulled up the file on your case before coming here, and the pathology report from your surgery has come back. It is very good and indicates that the cancer was contained to the tumor area with no spread to the lymph nodes. Dr. Matthews was able to get sufficient margin when removing the tumor, and the prognosis is very good. I am sure you have been waiting for this news."

I open my eyes to see him talking to Nancy, and I hear her start to ask him questions. The news has not settled into my head yet and for whatever reason, I am pissed off at this conversation between my wife and this new doctor in my life. I feel a surge of energy and start barking.

"Great. Now can you stop your fucking chit chat and get someone to give me something for pain?" This is obviously not the response either of them was expecting. They are both staring at me with blank faces. Dr. Tanadin touches Nancy's shoulder as he exits into the hallway as if to say "*Ignore him, he's not thinking straight.*" Despite my obvious displeasure, Nancy insists on driving home the good news.

"Did you hear what he said? I think that means that you are going to be ok. This is so great!"

I'm sure it is, and I will appreciate the news if I live through this hell I am going through right now. I'm not counting on it and still believe that death is overtaking my body. I have never felt this kind of full body toxicity before. I feel like I am decaying. Is that possible while you are still alive? What good is the positive pathology report if I am going to die laying here? I want to say these things to Nancy but just can't muster the will.

Dr. Tanadin returns with a small army of medical people. The nurse who impaled my chest with the port needle is by my side, and she is injecting something into a tube. Her voice is muffled through the surgical mask, but it is very soothing.

"I just gave you something for nausea, and now I am giving you something for pain. It should work right away and make you feel better, ok?"

She barely finishes her sentence when I feel a warm, tingling rush blanketing my body from my face to my toes. *This is awesome.* I can't tell if this is relieving my pain or just giving me a euphoric high that makes me forget about the pain. Whatever it is, I LIKE IT! I start to relax my muscles and lose the negative thoughts that were haunting me moments earlier. People are speaking around me. I don't know if they are speaking to me or not and I really don't care. I just want to hold on to the first good feelings I have had in a while. My muscles are almost numb now, and I know I am going to drift off to sleep. I hesitate, thinking that if I fall asleep I may not ever wake up again. It doesn't matter. I have to let it go.

December 2nd, 2012
5:00 pm

The two medical assistants wheel my bed into position and lock the wheels. This will be my new home for the foreseeable future. It is a private room, and it looks exactly the same as the room I was in 2 days earlier. It has been a rough day, but I am still alive. I've pushed aside the thoughts of death I had when I got here and just tried to get through each new procedure they have made me endure. The injection for the port, a very uncomfortable CT scan that almost resulted in my taking a swing at the med tech and now I am awaiting a nurse who will fish a tube up my nose and down my throat. Lovely. The Dilaudid has been flowing every 4 hours, and they just gave me the latest dose. I love this shit. I don't much care what they do to me when I am high on this stuff. I know this procedure is going to be unpleasant, but I am not concerned. *Bring it on.*

The nurse is young and pretty. *I wonder how many nurses they have in this place? Every time I turn around there is a new one caring for me.*

"Ok, Mr. Dan, let's get this done so we can get you some relief. I am going to use the thinnest tube possible, but it is going to feel really uncomfortable to you. Try your best to relax and we'll get this over with as quickly as possible."

When they flat out tell you it is going to be "uncomfortable" what they really mean is "*this is gonna hurt.*" I look at the apparatus on the tray in front of me and wish I hadn't. A long tube and some form of lubricant along with small packages of things that I can't identify. I have my head tilted back, and I can feel the nurse's cool, latex covered hand against my face and forehead. It takes her three tries with a lot of groaning and squirming from me before she is able to fish the tube through my sinus passage and down my throat with a final destination of my stomach. I fall back into the uncomfortable hospital bed and close my eyes from exhaustion.

"OH MY GOD. That is unbelievable!" Nancy is right by my bedside and speaking to the nurse. They are both looking at something behind me. *What the hell is unbelievable? What are they both staring at?*

"Honey, you cannot believe the crap that is coming out of your stomach." My wife says with an incredulous voice. Her tone tells me that whatever this is that she is looking at is a discovery that explains all of the horrible stuff I have been through today.

"What did you say he had again?" She is asking the young nurse who is obviously happy to have the chore of shoving a tube down my throat over with.

"It's called 'postoperative ileus.' It is when your bowels don't wake up and function after surgery" She has turned away from Nancy and is speaking directly to me now.

"Basically your gastrointestinal tract is paralyzed, and everything you eat is obstructed from evacuating from your body. So it builds up, and you get sick like you did today. We are pumping your stomach, and that should give your body a chance to recover. You'll be here for a while."

"I can't believe it is almost full!" Nancy says, again looking over my head.

"What are you looking at? *What* is almost full?" I say to my wife. She is grimacing and gives this little shudder indicating that she is looking at something terrible.

"The stuff coming out of your stomach is going into this big container, and it is almost full. It is beyond gross!"

Lovely. I assume this is what has been making me wrench my guts out all day. It must be pretty fascinating because Nancy hasn't taken her eyes off of it since it started.

What was the word she used to describe my problem? Ileus? I am trying to process what the nurse described, but my mind is fuzzy. *My bowels didn't wake up?* Why the hell did they send me home then? I wonder what they do to "wake up" my bowels. The whole concept seems weird to me, and I am too tired to figure it out. *I am sooo tired.*

"Honey, I think I am going to go to sleep now. It has been one helluva day." I am looking at my wife, and she finally takes her glare off of the container behind me and makes eye contact.

"Ok, well I'll stay for a little while longer, at least 'til I know you're asleep. Thank God we brought you over here when we did. I knew you were really bad when you told me to call an ambulance. I can't believe……"

My attention span is gone and as much as I would love to engage Nancy in conversation, my body and my mind just want to rest. The exhaustion of this day takes over, and I am out.

December 3rd, 2012

The doses of Dilaudid and anti-nausea medication have been coming steadily every 4 hours. It all must be working because I haven't felt nauseous, and I certainly feel no pain. I can't help thinking that the Dilaudid is becoming more of a guilty pleasure than a necessary medical prescription, but I worry that if I tell someone that they may take me off of it. Perhaps I would be in excruciating pain if I wasn't getting it? All I know is that the minutes after the nurse administers each dose are borderline euphoria. Just such a wonderful feeling of light, carefree relaxation.

The voices I hear are nearby. Men. Speaking in low tones. I have no idea what they are saying, and I debate with myself about whether to open my eyes or not. *Is it worth the effort?* I decide that my curiosity wins over my grogginess so I start to scan the room. Huddled at the foot of my bed are 3 men. Two wearing lab coats and one in a dress shirt and tie. He has long hair but looks familiar. So does the dark skinned guy in glasses and a white lab coat. *Doctors.* I try to remember which office they are from. I have seen so many freaking doctors over the past couple of months I can't keep them all straight. One of them sees that I am awake and shifts his posture toward the others to finish the conversation. Lab coat boys leave, and Doctor Long Hair comes up to me.

“I’m Doctor Stephens, I work with Dr. Matthews. If you recall, I was in recovery with you after surgery.” Oh sure… Like I remember anything from the recovery room.

“The CT Scan shows a small hole about the size of a pin head by the incision area.” He indicated that everything else looked fine. “The ileus made you so ill we wanted to be sure nothing was going on in the surgical area that could cause further complications. We are going to start you on antibiotics to prevent an infection, but I think everything else will clear up by itself. We discussed the possibility of repairing it surgically but concluded that it will not be necessary.”

Jeez. This guy talks like a medical text book. ‘*Repairing it surgically’?* Not necessary indeed. I’m not sure how I would react if one of these guys told me that I had to go in for another surgery. Damn. I sure hope he’s right. I want to ask about the hole and what caused it, but the drugs make me not care. As long as he is sure that the problem is going to solve itself, why should I?

As I try to contemplate a response, I look at where the Doctor was just standing, and he is gone. Almost as though he disappeared before my very eyes. *Was I dreaming?* I am really not sure. Whoa. This Dilaudid is powerful. I turn my head slowly and see that there is no one in my room. There is a faint light coming from the window. The drapes are closed, but it is obviously daytime. I look up at the clock on the wall in front of me. 8:20. A new day. A day that I did not think I would see. Twenty-four hours ago, I was sure that my time was up. Totally sure. I felt my body rotting and my mind shutting down. I worried about the aftermath of my demise. I wept for my wife and sons. I felt guilt. Sorrow. Fear. More emotions than I can describe. But now I am here. I am alive. My thoughts turn to what I heard Dr. Tanadin say about the pathology report. I can't recall the details, but I know it was good news. REALLY good news. I heard it. Nancy was happy. I can process it now, and it makes me feel stronger. I am generally optimistic anyway, but I am suddenly filled with joy. *Is it the drugs?* Maybe a little, but I think it is more a feeling that I won. It seems like I was losing about this time yesterday. Not just losing, I was convinced the game was over. I've never been so happy to be wrong about something I was so totally sure about. I am back in the hospital, I have a damned tube up my nose, and I don't feel strong enough to lift my head more than an inch or two, but I know I am alive. I just have to fight a little longer. Work a little harder to recover. There is more to do. More life to live. Better days ahead. I actually feel like God is giving me a second chance.

December 3rd, 2012
4:00 p.m.

The room is crowded, and I don't recognize where I am. It must be a party because everyone seems jovial and I hear the clinking of glasses and chatter. I am walking... almost floating, through the crowd. Why can't I see anyone's face? As soon as I get close enough, they turn away. Every one of them. No one will talk to me, and no one will look at me. Am I supposed to be here? I haven't seen a single face since I got here. I don't know whether to laugh at this or be afraid. I am leaning toward the latter. Someone has to look at me, but no one does. It is like they are programmed to turn away as I approach. I listen for a familiar voice that I can talk to, but everyone's voice blends together. Maybe no one knows me here. I need to get out.

I step into another room, and it looks familiar. The bright showroom lights and the white linoleum floor combine to make me squint my eyes from the glare. I still can't see any faces, but I know where I am. This is my dad's kitchen and bath business. Custom Crafters. I see the stairs I used to climb up to where his cubicle is. I am making my way up the short flight, and again, everyone's head turns away so that I can't see any faces. I see my dad's cubicle. I see the files on a rack, and I can smell the musty cardboard from stacks of banker's boxes on the floor.

The old fashioned calculator that he used to pound on with a speed that amazed me. The big leather blotter. The ash tray holding his pipe. I can smell that pipe. I realize I haven't been here since I was maybe 9 years old, but everything is so vivid. Dad isn't here, and I look around at the other people. No faces, but they are laughing. Are they laughing at me? Maybe I am not supposed to be in Dad's cubicle. I look across the open space and see the glass-walled cubicles lined in a row. I see the appliances displayed down below and the back of people's heads as they meander through the showroom. "Hey" Someone is talking to me. I turn my head, but no one is there. "Hey buddy, let's see how things are moving today."

As I open my eyes and feel myself emerge from the deep sleep, I realize that this was no ordinary dream. The voice is Dr. Nelson, and he is feeling around my abdomen. I can't take my thoughts off of the dream I just had. The colors around the room. The sounds. The distinct smells in the air. The clarity of the memory. *It was the drugs.* Whoa. That was intense but in a strange way very pleasurable. Almost like I went to another dimension.

No wonder people get completely hooked on stuff like this. Kind of scary. I'm glad I am under medical supervision, or I might be worried that I too could get hooked on the stuff. Of course, the medical supervision I am under are the same people who sent me home with this whatchamacallit "ileus" thing that damn near killed me. I am totally awake now thinking about it. I feel like blasting Dr. Nelson who continues to want to make jokes. *Why the hell didn't you know I had this before sending me home? 'Eat whatever you want' you told me.* He didn't mention the part about puking out my entire gastrointestinal system. I'm not sure I can trust anything they tell me now. The anger and frustration subside, and I look around the room. The sun is shining through the big window, but Dr. Nelson's big frame blocks my view. I am still feeling the effects of the drugs and can't stop thinking about the very bazaar dream. I feel the tape over my nose and remember that I have this tube shoved in there. It seems like it should be painful, but it's not. I wonder if they pumped all of that crude out of my stomach by now.

"Ileus baby. Nasty stuff." Dr. Nelson says as he pulls the stethoscope off of my belly.

"It wasn't fun doc. Not sure why you guys sent me home if this was going to happen."

Dr. Nelson chooses not to acknowledge my veiled accusation and rolls right into his next one-liner.

"We'll get those bowels moving. We're gonna pump until you dump."

What the hell does that mean? I know he is trying to keep things light but jokes about my bowels and pumping my stomach aren't exactly giving me the giggles. I want this dude to leave. Bring me a pretty nurse. Give me more drugs. Leave me alone.

"Get comfortable because you ain't going anywhere for a while. We should be able to pull the tube by tomorrow and then start you on a liquid diet. Do you like Scotch? Just kidding. It's a slow process, but you'll be back on your feet soon. Which reminds me. Once we pull the tube, you need to get up and walk as much as possible. Get things moving so that your body starts to function normally again. Got it? Ok, I'm outta here."

I hear his clodhoppers thumping across the floor as he takes big strides through the door.

"Thanks doc" I say almost instinctively. What am I thanking him for? Shouldn't I be pissed at him? Maybe the drugs are taking the edge off, but I somehow feel better having said thank you. Gratitude is one of the things I want to focus on for however much life I have left. In that brief moment, I am thankful that I am in this hospital and that I have just been examined by a doctor who (hopefully) knows how to treat me. Now, can I close my eyes and find my way back to Custom Crafters?

December 4th, 2012
7:45 a.m.

"Good mawning suh. How ah you feeling today?" Dr. Tanadin's voice and accent are unmistakable. He is standing in front of me like a towering statue, with thick glasses. He is reading a chart and holding the papers within 3 inches of his nose. His cologne is pungent, and I see he is dressed very casually. I suppose he is waiting for an answer to his question so I try to come up with something witty.

"I'd say I've had better days doc, how about you?" Not particularly witty but at least I have officially begun a dialogue. I have a lot of questions. This is the first real chance I have had to talk to a doctor about this fiasco so here goes. I need to organize my thoughts. I don't know how much time this guy is willing to spend in here with me, so I must prioritize my questions. I quickly try to come up with what should be most important but my mind is still fuzzy. *How did this happen?* Yeah, that should be what I ask.

"Am I going to be okay, doc?" Apparently, my vocal chords and my brain are not aligned.

"Yes, you are. You suffered from a symptom that is common after surgery. An ileus in the bowel which is a condition where the bowel is sleeping and does not function. It is common, as I said."

“I heard. Where are you from?” I guess I am now asking the first thing that comes to my mind. The accent and appearance obviously piqued my curiosity to the point where I wanted to know this more than all of the other questions I wanted to ask about my current condition.

“I am from Nigeria.” He says. *Nigeria? In Africa? No shit?* Hearing this opens up a whole new bevy of concerns. First, I don’t equate “Doctor” with “Nigeria.” This makes me feel a bit guilty but hey, this is my life. Doctor Matthews sent him so I guess I have to assume he is qualified. A *real* doctor. Besides, I don’t have much choice at this point.

With that, Dr. Tanadin is hovering over me with stethoscope in ears, and he is putting the cold silver disc on my stomach.

“I am listening to see if there is any movement in your bowels. Breathe deeply and hold your breath for a moment.” I do as instructed and wait for his prognosis.

“Very little, very little. It will probably take a few days and then we will introduce you to soft foods but only slowly. I expect you will be here for at least a week. Are you a basketball fan?”

He has turned from my bedside to see that there are highlights from the L.A. Lakers vs. Orlando Magic game. I am not really in the mood to talk about basketball and wonder why he asked me that in the middle of examining me. Not very doctor like.

"Yeah, I am. So when you say 'very, very little,' what does that mean? Are you saying that I still have this ileus?"

"You're bowels move at all times when things are normal. It will take a few days for yours to do that. Don't worry, we are taking care of it."

He is talking but still watching the highlights.

"Kobe Bryant is not as good as he once was." He says as he shakes his head. As if he has a vested interest in the future of the Lakers. Almost as if coming out of a trance, he turns to me and starts bellowing.

"You had a very rough time of it the other night my friend. When a man speaks so harshly to his wife... Well, I knew you were hurting badly." Dr. Tanadin lets out a nervous laugh and shows a smile. *I'm starting to like this guy.*

"I thought I was a dead man doc. Sorry I barked. Sorry about the language."

Dr. Tanadin doesn't smile or acknowledge my contrition. He just sorts of lets out a grunt and looks at me over his thick glasses.

"You're pathology report is very good. You have a good future. Your wife is strong, and I could see she was going to stay here by your side. Dr. Matthews is the best surgeon for these procedures. You are a lucky man."

Wow, that is a lot of optimism in a few sentences. Not just a bunch of medical gibberish. No hedging. I hate when they hedge. All too many times they leave you with unanswered questions. Giving ambiguous answers. Not this guy. He impresses me as a straight shooter. I like that.

"Indeed I am, doc. Thanks for everything you did. And are doing." I say feeling like I am bonding more with Dr. Tanadin by the minute.

"In Nigeria, you would have been left to die. You would have been seen as weak and sick which of course you were, but in Nigeria, the weak and sick are left at the side of the road to die. The healthy cannot be burdened. I hope you are really thankful that you live here in the United States, in a culture where people take care of others. Where there is a true healthcare system, even if it is not perfect. I hear Americans complain, but they know nothing of what it is that they complain about. This is a country that helps its people and that is why it is the greatest country."

I'm riveted listening to this man. He has passion in his voice. His brief commentary instantly makes me feel very fortunate. Very grateful. I want to hear more.

"Well I can tell you this, Doc, I sure am grateful you were around the other night when I was churning my guts inside out. When you said 'I am in charge now' I believed you. I really did think I was dying. I appreciate what you did then, and I appreciate that you are taking the time to talk to me now. Most doctors seem to be so busy that they can't spend more than 30 seconds with you." The sound of my voice rattles in my head, and it feels uncomfortable. I have that nasally sound like a person who is stuffed up from a cold, but I am sure it is the apparatus that is shoved up my nose and down my throat.

Dr. Tanadin is once again watching basketball highlights, and it sounds like he is talking to himself. Maybe he is talking to me but either way, I can't make out what he is saying.

He tells me about a patient of his who is refusing treatment because of their religion. I'm struggling to understand Dr. Tanadin because of his accent, but it is a subject that he is obviously very passionate about. He is animated and raising his voice from time to time which I thought was a no-no in the hospital. I get the impression that no one is going to "shush" him. The nurse comes in, and he is talking to her about the antibiotics that have been prescribed for me. It sounds like he just upped the dose and I worry that this is not a good sign.

"I have added more antibiotics so that you will avoid any possibility of infection. That would be a very bad consequence, and we must make sure that it doesn't happen. I will be back tomorrow, and we will see how you are doing."

"Thank you, doc. I'll see you tomorrow."

What an interesting cat. Something tells me that this doctor is special. Listening to him speak to me with passion and resolve makes me feel like this is a guy who became a doctor for all of the reasons that we HOPE people become doctors. It isn't about the money for him. It isn't about working for the insurance companies. My take on Dr. Tanadin is that he is a guy who actually cares about making sick people better. I am looking forward to his visit tomorrow because I want to know more about him. As hard as it is to understand some of the stuff he says, I want to listen to what he has to say. I want to know more about Nigeria. There's something I never thought I'd be interested in.

December 4, 2012

"You look like shit, my brother. What the fuck are they doing to you in here?"

My buddy Russ has such an eloquent way with words. Most people, normal people, would conclude that there is nothing normal about the way Russ and I communicate. It is a constant comedy act filled with one-liners and guttural references that make no sense to anyone but us. Even though I am in no condition to joke, I am pretty happy to hear the sound of his voice. As I open my eyes from a deep sleep, I simultaneously hear and see my best friend and my wife in my room. Nancy is giving a forced kind of laugh at Russ's comments, and I can tell she is a bit uncomfortable. I address her first.

"Hi, Honey. How did this guy get in here?"

"I found him downstairs flirting with the nurses." She says, again with kind of a forced sense of humor.

Russ has a controlled demeanor, but I know him very well. His face is strained as he looks me over and surveys my condition. He doesn't want to let me see his concern, but I do. I want to joke with him, but I don't have much humor in me right now. I'm groggy and this damned tube fished down my throat is annoying. *I must truly look like shit.*

As I try to work up a sincere smile, I think about how valuable my friend is to me. It is not lost on me that Russ has put his busy life on hold to drive 3 hours up here to visit with me and help my wife. He will most likely drive 3 hours back home tonight and resume his life tomorrow. Nancy and I have spoken many times about how to define a true friend. Russ is the embodiment of a true friend. Whatever I need, I can count on him. He is here. Many others are not and will not show up. Family. Others who purport to be my "friends" will pay lip service to caring. They will "keep me in their thoughts and prayers" but if I really needed them? They will be too busy or have some other excuse. Not Russ. Never. He has always been there for me in good times and bad. And he is here now. I want to try to express to him how much I appreciate it, but I can't find the words. Instead, I'll just try to yuk it up with him.

"You drove all the way up here to see this? Ya got nothing going right?" I try to project my voice, but I know it is weak and sounds nasal because of this obstruction in my nose. Russ still looks a little shocked at my condition but comes right back at me.

"I came up here to kick the doctor's ass for you. You sure as hell can't do it. You're down for the count right now. Here, I brought you some tea." Russ plops a brown bag full of tea bags on my tray. He is really into natural healing and thinks these exotic teas will do the trick. I'm not so sure and couldn't have any now if I wanted to.

"Seriously, how did this happen?" On the occasions when Russ and I are serious with each other, we connect perfectly, and this is a sincere question. I'm sure he has asked Nancy the same question ad nauseam, but he wants a better answer than she has been able to give him.

"They killed my bowels. I couldn't shit so everything started spewing out of my mouth. The fuckers damn near killed me."

"Lovely description." Nancy chimed in to express her displeasure with my answer. Russ is still looking pretty serious.

"Well, they didn't kill you and luckily you're in good hands here. I just need you to hurry up and get better. Jeez man, I haven't had anybody's balls to bust. You're the only one who understands me. I've been constipated. Constipated in your honor. I mean you gotta get better soon so I can shit." As weird as it sounds, this is a show of love from my best buddy. I can't see her, but I know Nancy is rolling her eyes.

"They got any hot nurses in here? Some of the ones I saw outside are kind of cute." Russ is back to the comedy act, and I appreciate it. He and Nancy agree to have dinner before he drives back home. He asks Nancy and I what we need. What he can do. He repeats his offer several times and says he can come back tomorrow if we need him. This is my best friend.

December 5th, 2012

I had the first decent night sleep since I've been back here. Thank you, Dilaudid. I think I feel a little better, but I know I am weak as hell. Regardless, I am full of adrenaline right now because I need to figure out how to do something special for my wife today while I lay here in this God- forsaken hospital bed.

Today is our 31st wedding anniversary, a day that Nancy and I take very seriously. I had bought her anniversary cards before I went in for surgery knowing that I might not be able to drive for a while after I got home, but I didn't think I'd be back in the hospital. Needless to say, I didn't bring them with me when the ambulance carted me back here puking my brains out. They are still in the Hallmark bag, hidden under my jeans in my closet at home.

I'm thinking very hard about the need to call Nancy before she comes to the hospital, tell her where the cards are, make her swear not to look at them and bring them to the hospital so that I can sign them and give them to her. *I hope I can write with all of these tubes attached to me.* I'm probably putting too much thought into this, but in a way, I like thinking about something other than my physical ailments for a while. I've been so laser focused on my fucked up body that I haven't been able to think about much else. Today being my anniversary feels like a positive distraction. It is a special chance for me to show my wife how much I adore her. We celebrated our 30th anniversary in Cortona, Italy. I surprised her by hiring a wedding service, and we renewed our vows in front of a big fireplace in the lobby of our beautiful hotel.

Each of our sons wrote about special memories they had growing up, and the lady who renewed our vows read them during the ceremony. Lots of happy tears. It was a memorable celebration, and I loved doing it, especially because it made Nancy so happy. Who knew that as we sat there drinking champagne and enjoying each other that I had a cancerous tumor growing in my gut.

If someone had told me then that our 31st anniversary would be celebrated from my hospital room, I would have never believed it. But here we are. Whoever said "*Life has its ups and downs*" had no idea how profound a statement that actually is.

This room and my condition don't seem very conducive to a celebration, but I have to make something happen. At least make sure Nancy gets the cards I bought. She will probably be impressed that I had the forethought to even buy them knowing what I was about to go through. *I have to call her and tell her to bring the cards with her!* I search the room for the phone that I thought I saw earlier. I think about my cell phone which used to be such a vital part of my day to day life. Trying to remember where it is, I realize that it wasn't one of the "essentials" that I grabbed when they were wheeling me out of my house on a stretcher the other night. I don't see the phone, but that doesn't mean it isn't there. I am afraid to turn my head too far because I have this stupid tube taped to my nostril. I've become very sensitive to not jostling anything that might come loose... Wire, a tube, whatever.

"Good morning! I am Hannah, and I'll be your nurse today. Did you get a good night's sleep?" My new nurse has a bright smile and a chipper attitude. I feel a sense of relief. I've spent enough time in here to know that every shift is a different nurse and as Forrest Gump says, they are like a box of chocolates...you never know what you're going to get.

"Hannah I need your help with something. Today is my 31st wedding anniversary, and I have to call my wife at 8:00. Is there a phone in here?"

"31 years? That is before I was born! That is so sweet. Congratulations! Your phone is right here, and I will move it over to the food tray for you. Dial 9 for an outside line. If I am done with my rounds by 8, I will come in and help you call her. It's so awesome that you've been married for so long and you are anxious to call your wife. I hope I get to meet her."

Hannah seems sincerely touched. I instantly like her.

"You will. It's going to be kind of weird because I bought her cards before my surgery and now I have to ask her to bring them here so that I can give them to her."

Hannah doesn't think this is weird, and she continues to smile as she takes my vital statistics and listens to my abdomen.

"Anything?" I ask, hoping that whatever the hell these people are supposed to hear down there is coming through the stethoscope loud and clear.

"Yeah. It sounds good. Don't worry about it. Let's just make sure you get to talk to your wife before she leaves without her anniversary gift."

Hannah leaves the room promising to make it back and "help" me call my wife. I think she just wants to hear what I say, but it doesn't bother me. It makes me feel good to know that this young girl thinks my fussing over my anniversary is cool.

Even though I don't really need any help, I would kind of like Hannah to come back when it is time to call Nancy. I look up at the clock, and it says 7:20. *I'll call her in about 45 minutes. Damn that seems like a long time.*

Time is different in the hospital. Being bed ridden slows the clock to a painful crawl. Left alone with nothing but my thoughts and perhaps some mindless TV is not something I am used to. Typically, my life is so busy that I sometimes think there simply aren't enough hours in the day to get everything done. When things get really intense, I long for time to just sit quietly and think. What would I think about during those times? Work? Money? The future? Now my thoughts are dominated by my health. The future I think about extends no further than today, maybe tomorrow.

There is something comforting about the limitations of those thoughts. When your life is at stake, everything else that used to worry you seems so much less important. Almost meaningless. An afterthought. Having a singular focus on surviving is very manageable.

Nobody is expecting anything from me right now. I don't have any deadlines (real or imagined) to meet. No pressure. It strikes me that so many thoughts that filled my head when I was well were about my perception of what life was all about. The things I worried about in the past defined much of my life. Now those things don't seem to matter. I am laying here, and there is nowhere I can go. My big distraction is how I am going to pull off a decent anniversary celebration to make my wife happy. I'll take it.

I must have dozed off, but I am awakened by her pleasant voice.

“Ready to call the Mrs.? It’s 8:45. I checked on you at 8, but you were snoring. I figured you would want me to wake you, I hope that’s ok.”

Hannah is my new buddy. I like her voice, and I like her enthusiasm. I feel like she is an advocate for me. I trust her. Wow…I’ve known her for like an hour and I already feel this way! If I have learned one thing up to this point in my life, it is to trust my gut.

Hannah actually dials the phone for me and pulls the chord around to my left arm. My right arm is tethered with tubes and wires.

“I’ll leave you alone.” Says Hannah but I can tell she wants to stay and listen.

“You don’t have to leave. I’m just going to wish her a happy anniversary and tell her where to find the cards. Nothing X-Rated, I promise. Not after 31 years.”

Hannah giggles and makes herself busy shuffling medical gear around the room and tidying up. I keep my promise and simply tell Nancy “happy anniversary” and walk her through where to find the cards I bought her. She expresses surprise that I was thoughtful enough to buy them before this ordeal, and that pleases me. She sounds rushed, and I let her go. Nancy has a routine, and it has been totally upended by all of this. She scoots down to see me in the morning, drives 20 miles to care for and feed her mom and then 20 miles back at night to be with me. All the while taking care of our household and keeping friends and family updated on my condition. The stress must be unbearable, but she is holding up incredibly well. She is truly amazing and once again I count my blessings that she is my life partner.

"I look forward to meeting her. You guys are so cute." Hannah is flashing that big smile again, and it makes me feel good that my marriage is giving her a lift today. These nurses must deal with all kinds of unimaginable stuff. You have to be a special person to go into this profession, and she has my admiration. She gives me something for nausea and tells me she will be back to check on me in a while. I wonder whether I still need something for nausea or if the medicine they are giving me for it is keeping it away. *Better to be safe than sorry.* Alone in my room, I am feeling a bit more upbeat this morning. Despite the circumstances, I feel like it is going to be a pretty good day.

December 5th, 2012
2:30 p.m.

After all of the anxiety about giving Nancy her anniversary cards, we exchanged them in my hospital room with the whole thing taking about 90 seconds. Still, Nancy is happy and remains pleasantly surprised that I was so thoughtful about buying her cards before my surgery. She and Hannah hit it off as I knew they would and Nancy has lectured me several times about how lucky I am to have such great people caring for me. We both agree that this hospital breaks the stereotype of a depressing, dingy institution. The people who have cared for me actually do seem to *care*. Almost on cue, Hannah comes in and presents Nancy and me with an anniversary card signed by all of the nursing staff. Amazing. It almost brings me to tears. I try to maneuver around the tubes and wires to give her a hug with my left arm. Nancy manages a much easier embrace, and Hannah is pleased.

"You guys are just so cute." She says. I know that is her way of expressing her admiration of us so I don't take it as condescending.

"It's time for your pain meds, and I need to check that belly Mr. C." Hannah is back to being a nurse, and she injects the needle into the tube that transports the pain meds into my bloodstream. I've become used to this routine now and know what to expect. In a few seconds, I will feel that warm, soothing wave traveling throughout my body. A ping of euphoria will enter my brain, and I will get groggy. It begins as I feel the pressure of Hannah's stethoscope on my stomach.

"Oh yeah, things are definitely getting back to normal Dan. I think tomorrow the doctor will start you on real food. Slow and easy, though." Hannah's voice fades. The light in the room fades. I am headed for la- la land. For a brief second I think about asking Nancy to hang around until I wake up but under the influence of Dilaudid nothing much really matters. I've found that happy place between sleep and drug-induced consciousness. *Damn, this stuff makes me feel good.* I think I'll doze a little...

The TV is too loud, and I hear Nancy trying to talk over it. I open my eyes, and there is a dark-haired woman in a blue business suit standing at the foot of my bed. She has her back to me, and I cannot see her face. Her perfume is strong but sweet smelling. I turn my head to the right and see Nancy speaking to her in an animated way. I can't hear what the woman in the business suit is saying back to my wife. Nancy's face is somewhat expressionless. She doesn't look concerned but she doesn't look like this conversation is particularly social either. Is this woman a doctor? Is she here to discharge me from the hospital? Hannah said my bowels sounded good and that I could probably start eating so maybe they are letting me go home! I am trying to shake off the grogginess from the Dilaudid and see who this woman is, but she won't turn around.

"Who's that?" I ask Nancy while staring at the woman in the blue suit. I expect the woman to look at me when she heard my voice, but she continues to look down with her back to me.

"Who's who?" asks Nancy as she looks at me over her reading glasses. She has a magazine open in her lap, and she is waiting for an answer to her question.

"This lady. Who is she and what is she doing" As I ask the question and turn to see if the woman is paying attention.....SHE IS GONE. *Why did she leave so quickly? I wanted to talk to her.*

"Honey, there is no one here but you and me. What are you talking about? You must have been dreaming." I feel a mix of confusion and anger which is probably reflected in my voice as I answer my wife.

"What are *you* talking about? She was standing right there two seconds ago, and you were talking to her. I saw you. Who was she?"

Nancy pulls the magazine off of her lap and almost darts over to my bed. She has a stern look on her face, and I worry that the woman in the blue business suit gave her some bad news.

"Are you awake? Can you hear me right now?" she says moving her face close to mine. Why is she doing this?

"Yeah, I'm awake. What's wrong? Did she bring bad news?"

"No one has been in here except you and me for the past hour. It was a dream. Either that or you're hallucinating from the drugs." Nancy is speaking loudly as if I might have trouble hearing her even though she is 8 inches from my face.

"Don't tell me that, I saw her. She was standing right there, and you were talking to her two minutes ago. I saw it. I was awake and saw you talking to her! It was not a dream." I am obviously agitated now. *It wasn't a dream....was it?* Nancy is having none of what I'm telling her.

"That's it. I don't think you need this much pain medication anymore, and it's making you loopy. You're seeing things for God's sake! I'm telling Hannah I want them to reduce your pain medication." Nancy moves toward the door like this is a matter of great urgency which needs to be addressed immediately. I let my head fall back to the thin hospital pillow and think she may be right. This shit is really powerful and between the dream I had yesterday and this apparent hallucination, maybe I need to dial it back. *My love affair with Dilaudid is going to have to come to an end.*

December 6th, 2012

Dr. Nelson has an unmistakable sound. His heavy steps. His breathing. That voice. I'll bet he is the life of the party if he ever gets invited to any. He tries to be jovial, but it seems forced. Still, I think I would prefer that over a doctor who is somber and non-communicative. As he barrels his way toward my bedside, I decide I am going to make the best of it.

"Hey, big guy, ready for steak and eggs? I don't think this liquid diet flowing into your veins has much taste." He looks at me to see if I laugh. I don't feel like laughing, but I muster a pretty hardy smile.

"I only want the steak and eggs if my bowels are ready to do their job. Nobody seems to want to tell me what they hear down there or if it is good or bad."

Without saying anything in response, Dr. Nelson puts his stethoscope on my stomach and stares down. He checks one or two spots in a matter of about 10 seconds, then pulls the stethoscope off and reaches for my nose. In one motion, he peels the adhesive tape off and quickly pulls the long tube out of my nose.

“Does that answer your question?” he says as he throws the tube onto a medical tray and turns the pump it was attached to off.

“Wow. That was easier than I thought it was going to be.” I said. That tube hurt like hell going in but coming out was a breeze. I feel an instant surge of relief, and I soak in the pleasurable moment.

“We are going to start you on liquids and soft foods for a couple of days to see how you do. Your body is going to need to adjust before you can eat anything solid. That should be later tomorrow or the next day. Once we see you passing gas and moving your bowels, we can talk about you getting out of here.”

“If I can pass gas and take a shit at the same time do I get extra credit?” I find myself in a joking mood now that I am free of the nose tube thing. Dr. Nelson lets out a sincere belly laugh.

“My 8-year-old son sharted in the pool the other day,” says Dr. Nelson. “I asked him what happened, and he said, ‘dad, I felt something coming on, so I gambled and lost.'”

I actually laughed and meant it. It was a good moment after the past few days, and I enjoyed sharing some levity with the good doctor. His smile faded, and he got a bit more serious.

"You need to start getting out of this bed and moving around. Walk the hallways as much as you feel like you can. Walking will help you get your strength back, and it promotes healing. It'll also get your bowels moving and you know that's a good thing. Ya wanna go for a walk now?"

This is something I feel like I should think about, but I quickly answer "yes." "I'll get the nurse in here to help you up and get you going. You're doing great champ."

And Dr. Nelson darts out the door.

What a weird guy. My thoughts turn to my new found "freedom" of having this foreign object removed from my body. It didn't really bother me as much as I thought it would but having it removed is definitely a small victory. I see it as a step back toward normalcy and hopefully it gets me closer to going home.

I can't wait to tell Nan that I got the tube removed. For the first time since I ended up back in here, I feel upbeat and optimistic. I can't deny the fatigue, but I really don't feel sick. I am not experiencing any pain from the surgery, and I can't help but wonder if that area has been quietly healing while I went through this new ordeal. Lots of good thoughts rolling around in my head and I like it. I think back to what Dr. Nelson said moments ago… '*liquids and soft foods*' I wonder what that means? I hope he knows what he is talking about. He said my bowels should do their job, but does he really know? *'Get out of bed and start walking.'* Getting out of this bed sounds like a helluva good plan to me. I've determined that there simply is no way to stay comfortable when you spend this much time in bed, especially one as thin and unsupportive as this one.

My butt hurts, my elbows feel scraped from trying to lift myself up and maneuver around, and my back is cramped. *Hell yeah, let's get out of this freaking bed and walk around.* I feel a burst of energy, and I am anxious to make this happen. The nurses call button is conveniently sitting right at my fingertips, and I decide not to assume that Dr. Nelson told her to come and get me. I push the button and wait for the voice to respond from the loudspeaker over my head.

"What do you need?" the faceless voice crackles from the cheap speaker.

"Can you send the nurse to help get me up? The doctor just left and said that I needed to get up." I figured if I dropped the "doctor's orders" thing on her she might feel a sense of urgency.

"We'll have someone there shortly honey."

I try to identify the voice to see if this was one of the nurses I have gotten to know. Not likely. Most of the nurses who have cared for me thus far are in constant motion. Not the desk driving types. I've learned to respect these women more than I could ever imagine. Admittedly I am a little picky about how I perceive medical caregivers.

I question everything, and my skepticism can make me kind of a pain in the ass. It hasn't gotten any better since I got back in here. I have tried not to think too much about the fact that I was sent home with this "ileus" condition which damn near killed me. SOMEBODY fucked up, that's for sure, so why should I trust any of these people? I don't know, but these nurses have made me feel like I am the only one they are caring for. Especially Hannah. I wonder if she is my day nurse today.

I don't have to think about it for long because I hear her voice just outside my door. I push on my sore elbows to reposition my body up in the elevated bed. I am ready to start my walk, and I am thankful that Hannah is going to help me. My anxiety kicks in when I don't see her coming into my room. *Maybe I can swing myself around and stand up on my own?* While I believe I can do it, my better judgment takes over, and I decide to patiently wait for Hannah. It seems to take forever, but she finally emerges from the lighted doorway.

"Oh my, I'll bet that feels better!" she says with a huge smile. I like this girl. I want her to marry my son. She is so sincere and pleasant. Her attitude makes me feel better.

"Free at last, free at last. Doc wants me to go for a walk. Can we make that happen?" Hopefully, this is a rhetorical question because I am really looking forward to getting vertical. A quick assessment of my condition tells me that I almost feel *good!*

"Let's do it Mr. Dan. I will help you up, and you can push your sidekick along as you walk. Don't overdo it but do as much as you can." She says as she lowers the rail at the side of my bed. I can't help but think that Dr. Nelson must have spoken to her based on what she just said.

I am surprised at how easily I swing my legs around and pull myself up to a sitting position. With very little effort my feet are on the floor, and I push myself up to stand for the first time in three days. My head gets a bit light, but I shake it off quickly. Hannah has her hand on my elbow and stands by my side to help me keep my balance With her free arm, she pushes the pole that holds the bags of fluids that are still being infused in me so that she can balance me while pushing the wheeled rack I am attached too. *Here we go.*

I have no pain and even though I know I am slightly hunched over, I feel like I could easily straighten up. Shuffling my feet I enjoy the forward motion and changing the scenery. When you are laid up in bed for days on end, the view never changes much. People come and go, but the landscape in front of you remains constant. I've never been too good at staying in one place for too long, and I am anxious to see what there is to see outside of this little room.

"Not too fast Dan, you're still getting your land legs under you. Let me know if you feel faint or start getting too tired." Hannah is holding me tighter than she probably needs to, but I'm not complaining.

"I'm good. Let's get the hell out of here." I am determined, and I start picking up speed. It feels good. Invigorating. *This is what getting better feels like Danny boy!* Passing through the doorway feels like entering a new world. The hospital floor is bright and alive with activity. As Hannah and I make our way out into the wide hallway, I expect everyone to look at me and possibly gawk at my condition. Either that or admire me for getting up and walking out here. No one does. Everyone is busy. I am just another patient. They've probably seen a zillion versions of me during their daily routine each day. I realize that while this is such a major life event for me, these folks deal with it every day. How do they not become desensitized to it? This is a big floor, and there seems to be an endless number of rooms. All of these people are in here for different reasons, none of them good. These skilled people deal with all of it. While I don't like thinking about it, I'm sure some of the patients they care for don't make it out of here. How do you go home to your family after dealing with that as part of your job? It makes me both sad and proud at the same time. I look over at Hannah as these thoughts race through my mind. She is still smiling. Holding my arm and we are sort of strolling.

"You rock young lady!" I just want to express some sort of extraordinary appreciation for this girl and the profession she represents.

"Aw shucks Mr. Dan. Seems like you're the one doing the rocking right now. You feel ok?"

"It actually feels great. How far should we go?" I ask her, realizing that even though I've only gone about 50 feet, I am starting to feel tired. My breathing is getting more rapid, and my knees are starting to get shaky. Hannah must sense this.

"What's say we turn around here and head back? You did awesome for your first time out of bed after this whole thing. We can walk further later, but it would probably be a good idea for you to rest up before we go again. When we get back, you can sit up in the chair, and I'll get you cleaned up a bit. Does that sound okay?" Hannah gently turns me around, and we start back toward my room. *Clean me up a bit.* Yes! That does sound good. I realize I haven't showered in about a week. I don't know what she has in mind, but anything that would make me feel fresher would be good.

"Okie Dokie. Let's go." I reply and start the trek back to my room. Every step gets more difficult. I might have overestimated my strength and gone too far for my first time out. I can see my room, and it isn't that far away. I feel more exhausted with every step, but I keep pushing until I walk through the door and back into the familiar little quarters that are my temporary home. I try to wrap the stupid hospital gown around my bare ass as I plop myself down into the chair. *Ahhh, this feels pretty good.*

"You just relax for a few minutes. I'm going to check on some of my other patients and get what I need to give you a bath. I'll be back in twenty minutes or so. Are you comfortable in the chair?" Hannah is looking me in the eye, and she probably sees that I am a little uncomfortable. It's not the chair. *Hannah is going to give me a bath?*

"How do we do this Hannah? The bath thing I mean."

"Oh, it's easy. I have a special body cleanser that we use. You don't even have to get up from the chair. It's fine. I'll be back in a few. Just sit there and rest."

I'm sure she senses my relief. As much as I have become fond of Hannah, I don't think I am ready to have her "bathe" me in the true sense of the word. Whatever she has in mind sounds pretty harmless, and I could definitely use a little freshening up.

As promised, Hannah returns a few minutes later with a tray full of small bottles and wash cloths. She applies the liquid to the wash cloth and starts slowly rubbing it over my head and neck. *This feels amazing.* The cool, cleansing liquid seems to evaporate on contact, and it is almost erotic the way Hannah moves it over my upper torso. I have my eyes closed, and I am almost purring at how refreshing it is.

"With all of the critical things we have to do every day, sometimes it's the simplest things that make the most difference to our patients. Like giving them a much-needed bath to make them feel better. I think that is what I like best about my job." I let Hannah's words soak into my brain. Not that I had any doubt before this moment, but I know this girl is special. I am so blessed to have her taking care of me. *I am getting better. One reason that I am is because of this girl.* I believe she knows this without me saying anything.

"Right on Hannah. I am actually starting to feel human again thanks to you."

My eyes are still closed, but I can feel Hannah's smile.

December 8th, 2012

I officially have a new friend. Dr. Tanadin has been visiting with me every morning and in addition to giving me the obligatory review of my current physical condition he spends time waxing philosophical about a wide range of topics from diet to politics and everything in between. Today is Saturday, and he is dressed casually. He has just examined me, listening to my belly and checking my chart.

"I think you will be going home by tomorrow. I want you to be eating well before you leave, but you seem to be tolerating it just fine. I will tell your wife."

Dr. Tanadin admires my relationship with Nancy. I can tell he sees the value in a strong marriage although he is not married himself. I find him to be a very interesting person. He is passionate about his opinions and wants to espouse them in great detail. This morning he is hammering the shortcomings of the hotly debated government healthcare system known as Obama Care. His accent is thick, and I always have to listen intently to understand everything he is saying, but I manage to get the gist.

"The government doesn't know how to manage themselves so why do they think they can manage our health care? The doctors will not be able to support their offices and students will no longer wish to become doctors because it will not afford them the living that it used to. The system will decline, of this I am sure. It will take time for the deficiencies to be revealed but the people will not stand for it over the long term."

He is not looking for me to respond, although I nod my head in agreement. His voice is a loud baritone and very animated in its inflection. He rambles for a good 10 minutes before I can say a word. When he takes a break, I take the opportunity to change the subject to something a bit more relevant to my situation.

"I am up and walking more than I am in the bed now doc. I did about fifteen laps on the floor yesterday and sat in the family lounge for a while taking in the view. I think the nurses are starting to wonder what I am doing here. I saw the sign in the elevator lobby that says 'Surgical PCU' and I assume that means that most everyone else on the floor is in a similar boat. I am starting to feel guilty that I might not need the attention now that I did a few days ago. I don't want to take time away from these other folks who are in need of more care."

Dr. Tanadin looks at me very seriously and delivers his point sternly. "PCU stands for Progressive Care Unit, and you have progressed yes, but you are not out of the woods my friend. You are not leaving here until it is the right time and that is my decision. Continue what you are doing and stop worrying. A man down the hall was shot last night, and the police are waiting to see if he survives so they can interview him. They are caring for him on this floor because it gives him the highest chance of survival. Be thankful that you are receiving the care you need and work to get stronger. You will go home soon, I assure you."

This guy is big on being in charge. Normally my nature would be to resist to some degree but not now. I need someone to be in charge and direct the action. Maybe if he had been in the picture after my surgery, I would not have been sent home, and this whole ordeal would never have happened. If I consider this for too long it pisses me off so I quickly let it go. The fact is that I feel better right now than I have since my surgery and lying in bed is getting old. I am able to get in and out of bed with little effort and certainly no help. I am walking a lot and not just because I was told that I have to. I want to be out of this room as much as possible, and I want to see activity around me. I feel alive and alert. I block out Dr. Tanadin's towering voice for a moment and fully embrace how good I feel right now. I don't feel sick anymore. I have fought my way out of the gloomy fog of being totally down for the count and emerged to the point that I feel like I am ready to get on with life. *Get on with life.* That thought drives deep into my heart and gives me a shot of sheer joy. A few short days ago I was sure that I was living my final moments. I was in the deepest chasm of despair. My body was failing, and I saw no future. No hope. Now I am ready to go home and truly get back to living. *I have a second chance to live my life.* I am anxious to get started.

Having my cell phone back is both a blessing and a curse. As dependent as I have become on this device, it was rather pleasant not dealing with it while I was sick. Most of the emails I have checked are spam, and I have a couple of well-wishing voicemails from acquaintances. I have heard from people that I would never have expected to hear from and not heard from people that I fully expected to hear from. I know that means something to me, but I don't want to process it right now.

People who thought enough about me to reach out are a blessing. People I didn't hear from probably have their reasons. Maybe they are not comfortable communicating with me under awkward circumstances. Maybe they are waiting until I get out of here, just being considerate. Maybe they don't know. Of course, there is always the possibility that they simply don't give a shit.

Regardless, this whole ordeal has made me reevaluate so many things. I expect that reevaluation to continue and include the people I most value in my life and how I will embrace them from now on. Maintaining the relationships within our lives is time-consuming.

The thought of dying really drives home the preciousness of time. I have the choice of whom I want to invest my time in, and I will invest more wisely in the future. I don't believe that is selfish, just efficient and emotionally prudent. If others think it is selfish, I don't care.

Time is too important to waste on people who don't bring value to your life or appreciate the value you bring to theirs. A few people come to mind. Some are my own blood, and that hurts me a bit, but reality can be like that. Some are people that have reached out to me, and I have failed to reciprocate. *I will make a point to remedy this and let them know that I care about them.*

One of those people is a former colleague named Steve who wrote me the most heartfelt letter. People I currently work with who have stayed in contact with Nancy and sent me flowers and cards here in the hospital. I don't even know them that well but they have been thoughtful enough to spend their time and money to let me know they are thinking of me.

Russ has been driving 200 miles each way and acts as if it is just around the corner. I sense that he wants to do so much more than he can. My sons are rocks of positivity. They have told me since day one that they know everything was going to be ok. I know there is worry within them, but they don't show it, and they have done their best to keep Nancy and me upbeat and positive throughout this ordeal.

My wife is tireless. She has been carrying the entire burden of our home, driving here to be with me and then driving to the assisted living facility to feed and care for her mother. There is a special place in heaven for people like Russ and the angel I call my wife.

Enduring a catastrophic illness forces you to refocus your life and what is important. People who actively care and those to whom you are an afterthought. How you use your precious time. What defines happiness? Many things that were reactive as I went through my day to day life before I found out I had cancer. Reactive in the sense that I did not think about them with any level of focus until something happened that forced me to.

My level of awareness is so much stronger now than it ever was and for that I am grateful. I don't know how much longer I have on this earth. No one does, I recognize that, but facing death to any extent simply makes you feel like you don't have that much more time. As I think of this, I recall a country song I've heard by Tim McGraw. *Live Like You Were Dying.* The essence of the song is that you need to experience life to the fullest extent possible every day because it may be your last. It stresses becoming a better person in the time you have left, knowing that the end is near. It is framed within a story about a terminally ill father giving advice to his son. It makes me cry. The reason it makes me cry is that it is an intense truth.

I want to live whatever amount of life I have left to the fullest. I want to be a better person and have a positive impact on the people I care about. I want to leave a legacy for my sons that they will be proud of. As I sit here in this hospital room thinking these thoughts, I feel a great sense of resolve that I will truly have a better life from now on. It is a choice that I am making right here and now. I know that I can do it and I will.

The steady buzz of my vibrating cell phone pulls me away from my deep thoughts. I reach over to the tray where it sits face down and looks at the screen. "Russ." I have a goofy picture of his face as the background for when he is calling. I swipe my finger across the screen to answer the call.

"Pizza Hut," I say, letting him know that I am in good spirits and ready for the never ending comedy act that we perform with each other on a daily basis.

"I'd rather eat the box," he says without hesitation. "Did you shit today so they'll let you out of that prison you're in?" My conversations with Russ have no beginning or end. They seem to be streams of spoken thought that we both understand perfectly.

"Yeah, the plumbing seems to be back in working order. Of course, it's not surprising since all I eat is grits and Jell-O. The coffee is awful. I'd kill somebody for a Starbucks right about now."

"Ya want me to come up there and bring you Starbucks? I'll do it, but you have to rub my feet."

Laughter is precious. It doesn't matter what makes you laugh, whether it is something that just hits your funny bone or something as silly and ridiculous as what Russ just said to me. It's the feeling that bubbles up from somewhere within you that results in the outburst that we call a laugh. I've read a few things about the health benefits of laughing and generally I believe it.

Russ and I laugh often. I think it is our therapeutic gift to each other. We say some of the most childish, insanely silly, goofy, nonsensical stuff to one another. Anyone who would hear the things we talk about very well might suggest that we enter a psychiatric institution. But under all of the silliness is goodness. The insanity of our dialogue keeps us sane in a crazy life. Laughing is our defense mechanism, and we use it freely.

"Your feet are more disgusting than the crud they pumped out of me, and I'm never touching them. I'll get my own freaking Starbucks in a couple of days so rub your own fucking feet. Seriously, I'm way ready to get out of here. My butt cheeks are chapped from the plastic bed sheets and this vinyl chair. It's been a lovely stay, but I am ready to go home." I'm whining, but it is true.

I feel no more worry about going home like I did a few days ago. I am confident I can take care of myself well enough to keep from being a burden on Nancy. I have walked around this floor more times than I can count and my stomach is tolerating food. I still get tired but not as quickly. I want to do things that make me feel alive and right now I can only think about being at home. Trying to start a new life without all of this worry.

"Well did the doc say you could get out today? I can come up there if you need me." This is an offer my buddy has made dozens of times over the past few months, and I know that he means it.

"He was here this morning and said it will probably be tomorrow. He hung out with me for almost an hour. He's my new official doctor."

"So you have to tough it out for one more night. There ya go. Tomorrow you'll be back in your own bed. I'm sure Nancy hates that idea. She's probably been loving the fact that she hasn't had to deal with you farting on her every night, ya pig." The humor never stops.

December 8, 2012
11:30 a.m.

Nancy had said she would be here around noon. I am very antsy now so I decide to walk around the floor again, stopping at the family waiting room. No one is in here so I walk to the window and take in the lovely view. It is a bright sunny day, and I can feel the warmth coming off of the floor to ceiling glass window. This room is less stark than the rest of the floor, with a dark blue carpet and ambient lighting. Family members wait here as their loved ones are treated in the rooms that line the sterile hallways where I have spent so much time walking this past couple of days. I can imagine the extraordinary stress that this room has held, and it makes me uncomfortable. *Enough of the view.*

I walk briskly out into the bright hallway and glance toward my room. I see Nancy walking into the room. I have noticed that I feel a sense of pride when I know that Nancy sees me functioning more normally. I believe it gives her confidence that I am recovering and will soon be able to care for myself. Hell, maybe I'm already there. I kind of feel like if they would get these last few tubes and wires out of me, I'd be fine without them. *Patience. Just a little bit longer.* I am heading toward my room to get as close as possible before Nancy emerges. I don't close the gap by much before I see her step out and walk toward the main nurses' station. She doesn't even glance my way so I have to keep schlepping, even further now to the nurses' station. She is standing at the counter speaking with someone who is out of my line of sight.

As I walk toward her, a big man in scrubs turns the corner blocking the view of my wife. He is talking on a cell phone, and I recognize him immediately. It is Dr. Nelson, and we make eye contact. He is making facial expressions at me while continuing to talk on the phone. Somehow Nancy must have seen me as well because I see her walking toward me a few steps behind Dr. Nelson. *Oh cool, we're gonna have a party in the hallway.*

"Lookin' good there my man! At this rate, you'll be out of here in no time. Do you feel as good as you look?" The guy always seems upbeat, I'll give him that.

"Yeah doc, I'm feeling much better. Aren't you going to ask me if I pooped or farted or threw up or something else disgusting?" I am trying to speak loud enough for Nancy to hear also. If I am joking around, she will know that I am in good spirits. It must work because I hear her familiar giggle and see her smiling face.

Dr. Nelson and I come face to face. The three of us stop in the hallway to talk. Dr. Nelson barely acknowledges Nancy and turns to answer my question.

"Well, you tell me. How are the bowel movements now? Your bathroom habits are going to change from now on. Sometimes you might go 9 times in a day. Sometimes you might go a few days with nothing. No need to be concerned. You'll get used to it. Did you go today?"

Jeez doc, it was a joke.

"No, but the day is young. There is talk of me getting out of here. Do you have any information for me on that?"

"Looks like you're ready to go home. Can't blame you. I'm thinking tomorrow." Dr. Nelson now turns to face my wife who has been listening intently to this exchange. "Are *you* ready to let this guy back in your house? He looks a helluva lot better than he did the first time we handed him over to you."

Nancy lets out a little chuckle but directs her answer to me.

"I think I can handle it. No big parties, though."

I'm not sure Dr. Nelson even heard her because he started talking before she finished her sentence.

"I'll get everything arranged, and if you are still in good shape tomorrow, we'll spring you. Hang in there big guy. See you in the office next week. We'll get those staples out of you. No needles, I promise!" His voice fades as he scurries down the hallway and into another patient's room.

"I'm sorry, he's weird," Nancy whispers to me. She gently takes hold of my elbow and asks me how I am doing. Even though we are in the midst of the hustle bustle of the hospital, I feel like the two of us are alone together. We start walking together back toward my room, and I am glad to know that I have a change of scenery in my not too distant future.

I think to myself that it would be really nice for Nan and me to start taking leisurely walks together at home. Even when I am all better, the walking is good for both of us, physically and mentally. *Make that part of 'the new me'.*

A nurse I've never met is in my room when I return. Her name is Alex and like so many of the nurses who have cared for me, she is a ray of sunshine in this otherwise dark place. Alex has the usual tray of unidentifiable medical gear that she is fiddling with. She is smiling before she even looks up to see us entering the room.

"You are a walking machine, Dan! I think you will be walking right out of here pretty soon. Dr. Nelson just told me you are out of here tomorrow. That should make you happy." She turns to my wife and her smile widens.

"Hi, I'm Alex." She says with an outstretched hand. Almost immediately after shaking Nancy's hand she pumps the white foaming hand sanitizer from the canister on the wall.

Those things are hanging on the walls about every ten feet throughout the hospital.

Proper handwashing is taken very seriously, although I have had enough of the smell. I think my senses have been heightened in here, and that is not necessarily a good thing. The smells are particularly unpleasant, and I am looking forward to some fresh air. Even the food smells unnatural.

I hear the familiar clanging of the food carts outside my room and know that my lunch will be in front of me soon. I am finally eating some solid food although very small portions. Grits with butter are my new delicacy, more because it feels safe than because I enjoy the taste.

Alex has my medication which I wonder is even necessary at this point. Three pills in a tiny paper cup. I heave them back and drink the entire cup of water. Alex and Nancy are chatting about the weather and Christmas. Nancy seems relaxed and happy. She and Alex are hitting it off which has been the case with most of the nurses I have had the pleasure of meeting over the past couple of weeks.

"Dan. I will most likely be your discharge nurse tomorrow, and I will go over everything with you before you leave." She turns to Nancy and is speaking with an authoritative command of the room.

"Nancy, I would like you to be here so that you both understand everything, especially since you will be caring for Dan at home. Dan, you are not completely recovered, and that is perfectly normal. Your body will continue getting healthier every day."

The reality that I am actually going home tomorrow sets in with Alex's final words. I am excited and nervous at the same time. I think of how uneasy I was about going home after surgery. My instincts were telling me that it was too soon. I was right. This time, I am confident that being at home is the right thing for me. I am longing for normalcy. I want to start living the life that I have been redesigning in my mind. I am alive and getting well.

December 9th, 2012

6:00 a.m.

I have no recollection of what time I fell asleep last night. I don't even remember Nancy leaving. No one came in during the night to check my vitals or give me medication. I didn't even get up to use the bathroom. I slept all the way through the night. The sun is not up yet, but I feel great satisfaction that I transitioned from night to day in a typical fashion. My head is clear, and I feel like I could hop out of bed and get my day going just like I did before my surgery.

I wonder how that would go if I actually did it? To think that a few short days ago I was convinced that my life was coming to an abrupt end seems like a distant memory. Dwelling on those hours of agony still makes me shutter, though. I take a moment and soak up the gratitude.

I look to the heavens and thank God for pulling me out of the abyss and giving me the strength to make it to this day. The depth of my gratitude makes me emotional, and I feel the tears welling up in my eyes. I didn't realize before how truly precious life is and how much I wanted to live.

This experience also helped me to focus on the things that are truly meaningful in my life as well as realize the things that are unimportant. I wouldn't wish the physical and mental pain of dealing with cancer upon anyone, but the crystal clear perspective on life that emerges from it is priceless.

I look around the room and see the faint gray glow of light protruding from behind the shades of my hospital window. Tomorrow morning I will awake in my own bed, and that simple thought gives me indescribable joy.

It is very quiet outside my room, and I am sure most of my fellow patients are still sleeping. I, on the other hand, am wide awake and ready to take on this very exciting day. *I'm getting up. There's nothing to stop me from taking a nice walk down the hall. Maybe my last one.* Swinging my legs out of bed and getting to my feet is almost effortless now but I still do so gingerly.

I take a moment to adjust to being vertical and then push myself up to my feet. Rolling the IV rack alongside me has become almost natural, and I start scooting toward the door. As I slowly swing the door open, the bright light of the hallway makes me squint. I hear absolutely nothing outside. I see no one. *This is a little eerie.* The door latches to the magnet that holds it open, and I venture out into the empty hallway. I feel that I am standing tall and straight, and I like it. I know right where I am going and start walking there at a brisk pace.

A few health care professionals appear from around corners, and I see them working at their stations, but no one is paying any particular attention to me. I smile and say good morning when I see someone within earshot and get a casual mumble in return. That's ok. This is just another day at work for them. For me? This is the day I start my life over again.

The lights are off in the Family Waiting Room that I have visited so many times in the past few days. The only light coming through is the rising sun from the floor to ceiling window that overlooks the pond and commercial buildings. That window is my destination.

My feet feel the transition from linoleum tile to the soft carpet of the Family Waiting Room. The vending machines are humming, and the room is completely empty. As I approach the window, I grab one of the chairs in the room and turn it to face directly out of the window. I carefully drop myself down into the soft chair and prepare to enjoy the sunrise.

By most people's standards, this sunrise would be very disappointing. No beautiful ocean or majestic mountain to serve as a scenic landscape from which the sun slowly rises above. No, what I see is a basic view of suburban Orlando with its mix of homes and commercial buildings. As the sun breaches the horizon, a yellow hue overtakes everything I see.

I am immersed in the wonder of this moment and very aware of how much I appreciate it. Gratitude is the new foundation of my life. I hope I can hold on to it as I leave this place that has given me such a wide range of feelings both physically and emotionally.

It has been a life changing experience. I don't know what the future holds, but I know I won't be the same. I am ready to start. The sun is up, and everything is looking much brighter.

December 9, 2012

1:30 p.m.

Alex has just left my room after removing the heart monitor that has been affixed to my body for the past week and a half. The "nodes" from the heart monitor did a number on my chest hair, and the sting lingers.

I've certainly felt worse pain in the past few weeks so I shake it off without much thought. I didn't realize how much the heart monitor weighed down my stupid hospital gown. After all of this time, it actually seems to cover my body as it is meant to.

Alex explains that a "specialist" will need to come in and remove the needle from my port. I remember from the first time. Nancy isn't here yet, and I am getting anxious. I am sitting in this chair next to my bed and make a decision that I will not get back into that bed. EVER AGAIN. In addition to the rising anxiety, I wonder about the removal of this needle. It wasn't bad the first time so hopefully I'll have the same result.

Alex said it has to be "flushed" and I am not sure what that means or how it will feel. *No sense in worrying about it, it's going to happen no matter what. I can handle it.* My thoughts turn to Dr. Matthews's mention of chemo, and my heart starts to race. If the pathology was so freaking great why do they still think I'll need chemo? I make a mental note to talk to him about it when I go to get the staples out. That happens tomorrow.

I think about calling Nan and asking when she will be here. I decide against it because she will think I am rushing her and it might upset her. I don't want to do that. *But I want to get out of here too!!!*

My quasi-trance is broken by the rumble of a large utility cart being pushed into my room by a middle-aged, redheaded woman in scrubs.

"Hello sir, I'm Melinda, and I am here to flush your port before you're discharged. How are you today?"

Melinda has a pleasant but businesslike demeanor. I answer with some trepidation.

"Good, but ready to blow this popsicle stand. Are you going to help me do that?"

My response generates a much more personable smile from Melinda who is not making eye contact with me. She is focused on the items on the cart in front of her. I can't see everything that is on there, but maybe that is for the best.

"I hope this doesn't feel as bad coming out as it did going in," I say with obvious nervousness in my voice.

"Not at all. We'll have it out of there in no time, and you should feel no discomfort in the process."

Good answer Melinda. Let's get this done and I am one step closer to getting out of here.

Melinda unties the back of my gown and pulls the front down to reveal the focus of her work. I look away because I don't know if I want to see what she is going to do. It's just safer to look at the TV. I feel the slow tugging of the adhesive as she pulls it off of my chest.

"Oh, Sorry," Melinda says as she can hear the sound of my chest hairs being plucked away. She performs a few tasks with the tubing and out of the corner of my eye I see her injecting something through the port. *This must be the flush.* I wait for some sort of sensation resulting from it, but it never comes. I am just beginning to feel relieved that this step in my discharge process is over when suddenly...

"AAAAGGGHHH" It feels like a knife has been thrust into my chest. The pain is sharp and excruciating. I gasp and squeal at the same time.

"Oh, oh, oh. What? I'm so sorry!" Melinda seems completely surprised at the reaction. She pulls away quickly and unlike a few minutes ago, is now looking straight into my eyes.

"Holy shit that hurt!" I said with no pre-thought.

"It may have been my thumb on the port. I'm so sorry. I didn't mean to hurt you… and after I just told you that you wouldn't feel any pain. I'm so sorry."

While Melinda's sincerity is evident, I really want her to get the hell out of here right now. That hurt like hell and I wasn't expecting it. As I open my eyes, I see her tidying up her tray and continuing to apologize. I think she wants to get out of here too.

"Is it out?" I ask, feeling as though I already know the answer.

"Oh yes. We are all done. I'm really very sorry about the pain. That is very unusual."

Unusual. Swell. Lucky me.

Melinda has now left my room, and I have recovered from the pain she inflicted. For the first time since coming back here, I am completely untethered. I stand up straight and soak in the reality that I am physically and mentally ready to get back to living my life. I look out the window and let out a big smile. I have a bevy of emotions, but my description of how I am feeling comes to me in one word. ***Victorious***.

Without dwelling on the details, I know I have overcome a great deal since that horrible day on October 4th. I truly believe that I have beaten this, although only time will tell for sure. I watch the movement of cars and people outside my window and think about a time in the not too distant future when I will be amongst them.

Staring down, I am almost hypnotized inserting the vision of myself functioning normally. My daydream is interrupted by the ping of my phone on the tray next to my bed. It is a text from Nancy. "On my way" along with a smiley face emoji. I think my time here is just about done.

December 9, 2012
3:15 p.m.

I look into the bathroom mirror and can't decide if I look good or bad. I just shaved and combed my sparse hair. My face looks thin but pretty average otherwise. I am saying goodbye to this God forsaken hospital gown once and for all as I change into a pair of sweatpants and a long sleeved tee shirt.

My movements are still somewhat measured and ginger but I think it is more out of habit now than pain. I assess my body and declare to myself that I am pain-free. I get winded easily, but maybe that is just the excitement of the moment. I slide the tee shirt over my head, and I am now officially dressed for my ride home.

I glance back into the mirror and smile at my reflection, as if to say *There damn it! We did it!* I am still smiling as I open the bathroom door and present myself to my wife.

"I'll bet that feels better, huh. Any problems changing?" Nancy is looking me up and down as she speaks. "Piece of cake, and yes, I feel human again," I say.

Nancy's words start coming rapid fire, but I love the sound of everything she says. "You've lost a lot of weight. Alex told me she would be back in a few minutes to go over some last minute instructions for us to do at home. She already called for the wheelchair. You have to leave in a wheelchair. I valet parked the car, but they said they would leave it up front so we wouldn't have to wait."

I walk as naturally as possible back over to my chair and sit myself down. Nancy immediately takes my hand in hers. This woman is so good to me…so precious. She isn't looking at me, but I am staring deeply into her face. How could I have survived this without her by my side? I am silently overcome with love and gratitude. I think about saying something to her, but instead, I just squeeze her hand a little tighter.

Alex has a bounce in her step as she enters the room. She is holding a handful of papers and a plastic bag full of pill bottles.

"Ok Dan & Nancy, I want to go over a few things with you before you go home. Here are the remaining prescriptions for the meds you have been taking. The names of the medications and directions for taking them are in the bag.

When you run out of something, first check with the pharmacy and see if it has already been called in. If not, give Dr. Tanadin or Dr. Matthews's office a call." She hands Nancy the bag and begins to address the papers she is holding.

"I printed out some information about the port you have. You were asking me how it works, and it is all explained here. You can have it in for a long time, up to two or three years with no problem. When the doctor tells you that you no longer need it, he will schedule a surgery for you to have it removed. I'm sure he will order annual colonoscopies for you so maybe he can do both procedures when you have the next one."

Alex very thoroughly explains how my port was inserted and how it functions. I am listening but wondering if I really need to know this. I did ask her how it worked earlier, but it was just out of curiosity. I am touched that she took the time to research it, print the information out for me and give it to me as I leave. She is just another shining example of the special people who have cared for me here. I commit to myself that I am going to write a heartfelt letter to the nursing director here expressing my gratitude for these awesome individuals.

Alex is still talking to Nancy, telling her that even she was not aware of some of the nuances related to how the port functioned. A young man rolls a wheelchair into the room behind her. Alex looks at me and smiles.

"Ok, it looks like you're good to go," Says Alex. She points to the orderly and introduces him as Charles. She informs me that Charles will be wheeling me to the lobby.

"Have you checked to make sure you have all of your personal items from the room?" asks Alex. She glances over at the large white bag that Nancy had brought which now holds whatever stuff I had when I was admitted so unexpectedly almost two weeks ago.

"Anything I forgot is all yours Alex," I say as I reach out to give her a hug. Alex hugs me back with caution and gentleness. Nancy also says her goodbyes. As I sit down in the wheelchair, I take one last look around the room. The medical professionals of this hospital cared for me both physically and emotionally and played a significant role in saving my life. But I can honestly say that I hope I never see the inside of this room again.

"Get me outta here Charles." With that, I am rolling briskly toward the elevator. As we descend the 14 floors to the lobby, I think about the importance of this place. It is so big, and I feel so small at this moment. I am just one of the millions of people in this world who are dealing with countless types of health issues. There are trained and caring professionals here who specialize in all of those different types of conditions and they are using their skills to treat those patients. Tomorrow all of the fellow patients that I shared the 14th floor with will wake up in their rooms and deal with another day of suffering and recovery. Tomorrow all of these skilled caregivers will show up for work and care for their patients for the purpose of moving them closer to a day when they also can go home. I will wake up in my home, next to my precious wife and I will begin anew.

December 9th, 2012
4:30 p.m.

The air is cool and crisp as I sit with my wife on our patio. I look into her face, and I see comfort. We are home together, once again enjoying each other's company in the place where we feel most comfortable. We designed this house together, and I built it to include everything that Nancy wanted.

The presence of our family is what makes this house a home. The house is not a home without us in it. This journey has been the toughest thing I have ever faced in my life, and I think Nancy would agree. I realize that the painful challenges we have endured together over the past two months make this moment indescribably special.

I have learned a new way to view my life. My loving wife has been my rock and stayed strong and positive throughout the fear, pain, suffering and angst. I can never repay her for what she has done for me, but I am happy to devote whatever life I have left to trying. I scan my surroundings and silently thank God for my blessings.

Two months and one day ago I sat in this very chair on my patio and saw the most beautiful red cardinal. I chose to believe that I was given a sign in the form of a bird that I had never seen before and brought me fond memories of my mother. I chose to see it as a positive sign.

I reflect back on that day and think maybe, just maybe, that cardinal was coming by to tell me that this moment was in my future. I look into my back yard and wonder where that cardinal is now. I don't see the cardinal, but I see a future. A few short weeks ago I had my doubts about whether or not there was much future left for me. But now I am optimistic, and I am ready. I am ready to get back to living, ready to be a better man, and ready to start living out my second chance.

EPILOGUE

The days following my return home were filled with determination. Recovery was slow, and my body had been ravaged by the prior weeks in the hospital. I was 38 pounds lighter than the day I went in for surgery, and I had to work to get my strength back. I walked around my neighborhood several times a day and even started back to the gym, all of which had its challenges.

One day I ran into an old friend while I was picking up something for Nancy at Target. He saw me and gasped. I told him about my ordeal, and his reaction was one you would expect from someone who had just been told that the person in front of them was dying. I went through months of hearing people tell me how good I looked and how thin I was. I vowed to focus on my health more than ever.

Chemo never happened. I set an appointment with an Oncologist, and he told me about a test that could be done *on the tumor* that would give them a pretty accurate indication of the likelihood that the colon cancer would reoccur. It blew my mind that they actually keep the tumor but the fact that a test such as this could tell me whether or not I needed chemo was a blessing.

After waiting a month for the results of the test, the oncologist recommended against chemo. He said that my risk of recurrence was between 3% and 8%. He said that at my age, chemo would pose a greater risk of leading to leukemia within the next 10 – 15 years and any potential benefit related to killing cancer cells would be lost against that risk.

I got very serious about my nutrition, but over time let my taste buds get the better of me again. I gained back most of the weight but not to the point where I was overweight.

Dr. Matthews continues to be my doctor, and I have seen him pretty regularly since the surgery. Two years after my initial surgery, he found another pre-cancerous growth in my colon during my colonoscopy. He was concerned but successfully removed it with another surgery. He still busts my chops about my fear of needles. According to him, he made my ordeal into a case study that he uses when he lectures and trains other surgeons around the world to conduct the kind of surgery he did on me. Once when I was in his waiting room, he saw me from down the hall and shouted "Hey Colachicco…I showed your rectum in Chicago last week!" It should have been an embarrassing moment, but I rather enjoyed the attention from him.

Dr. Tanadin and I have become friends. He is a special guy. He is one of the hardest working, tireless professionals I have ever known. He is my primary doctor and has treated me regularly since my surgery, but first and foremost he is a valued friend. His wisdom of the world and appreciation for the important things in life are things I have learned much from.

I wrote the letter to the Director of Nursing and named every single nurse who cared for me while I was in the hospital. It was seven pages long. I sent a copy of it to the CEO of the hospital. Every December since my hospital stay, I go back to the 14th floor. I bring Christmas cookies for the nursing staff. I've not seen any familiar faces in the times that I have visited, and the Director of Nursing is no longer in that position. I don't care. I just want to revisit and offer some small token of my appreciation for the amazing human beings who do this job every day. It is something I intend to do every year for as long as I am able.

November 27th ***2015***
10:08 a.m.

At this moment 3 years ago, I was consumed with an uncertain future. I had a cancerous tumor in my rectum that was about to be removed by what I hoped was the most skilled surgeon who specialized in such things. I had been working the rest of my life around preparing for the surgery that would tell me the likelihood of recovery or the possibility of an early death. What I was dealing with exactly three years ago at this moment is the kind of thing that people dread to the point of finding it almost unthinkable. I suppose I felt the same way until I actually did have to deal with it.

Fortunately, I was blessed with a second chance at life. As I sit here on my patio writing this, I am cancer-free. Life is good. I am a survivor, and I am thriving.

My loving wife and two precious sons were beside me at the table last night as we had a terrific Thanksgiving feast. We laughed, drank some wine, and got silly. I looked at these incredible gifts that are my family, and I silently thanked God for them and for all of the moments of the past three years.

I reflected back in time to Thanksgiving of 2012 and remembered pleading with God for the chance to have more Thanksgivings with my family; more time to cherish the ones I love. God answered my prayers and on this day after

Thanksgiving, 2015, my gratitude runs deep, and I am thankful as a man can be.

The lasting effects of my surgery were minimal, and I am now living a full and active life. My career is back on track, and our home is once again stable. Never a day goes by that I don't thank God for my second chance and for my loved ones. Every day is precious. It sounds cliché, but gratitude actually does help your attitude. Be thankful. Live every day of your life so that it counts. You may not get a second chance.

Acknowledgements

First and foremost, to say “thank you” to Nancy doesn’t even begin to express my gratitude. You are intertwined within the pages of this book and what’s written reflects a mere fraction of what you did for me through this ordeal. I love you honey. My wonderful sons, Billy and Anthony. I am so proud of you both and you played such an important role in supporting me and mom while I was sick. I love you both with all of my heart and soul. During the times that I needed to have my spirit lifted, Russ made me laugh and gave me hope. You are truly my brother and my gratitude for having you in my life is boundless. Mike Mollica, you are the most trustworthy guy I have ever met. Thank you for carrying the burden of responsibility that I entrusted in you. All of the nurses that cared for me, Matt, Samantha, Angel, Tammy, Madelaine, Hannah, Dulce, Eliza, Jessica, Nina, Luana, Mani, Alex and the many more that I did not know by name. You are amazing people and gave me amazing care. Ann B., Director of Nursing who took charge and assured that I had everything I needed. My editor, Jan Steele who made this book readable and as a nurse herself, made me feel that this book could be helpful to others. Thank you Jan. Starbucks and my barista friends Kirk, Em and Daniele who unknowingly witnessed me writing much of this book while keeping me happily caffeinated. My friends at Starwood who encouraged me leading up to my surgery, Jake, Stephanie, Harolt, Kez (RIP), Dawn and Vaike. Dave Patchin who took the time to visit me in the hospital and encourage me. Barbara Peckett who cares for Nancy like a sister and who was by my wife's side throughout this ordeal. You are family, Barbara. Christie Alexander who taught me the importance of celebrating every day of being cancer free. Gale M., my nutritionist who helped me learn how to eat properly after surgery. Sheila who got me the appointment with Dr. Matthews via text. Dr. Matthews, Dr. Nelson, Dr. Morrey and the staff at The Colon and Rectal Cancer Treatment Center. I can't imagine having more skilled professionals caring for me. All of the doctors that gave me my second, third and fourth opinions. Dr. Tanadin who saved my life and taught me a new appreciation for what I have in it.

www.ingramcontent.com/pod-product-compliance
Lightning Source LLC
LaVergne TN
LVHW011219080426
835509LV00005B/217

* 9 7 8 0 6 9 2 0 3 3 9 1 3 *